Memoirs and Reflections

Memoirs and Reflections

EVGENY KISSIN
Compiled and edited by Marina Arshinova
Translated by Arnold McMillin

ForeEdge

ForeEdge
An imprint of University Press of New England
www.upne.com
© Evgeny Kissin and Marina Arshinova 2017
English translation © Arnold McMillin 2017
All rights reserved
Manufactured in the United States of America

For permission to reproduce any of the material in this book,
contact Permissions, University Press of New England,
One Court Street, Suite 250, Lebanon NH 03766;
or visit www.upne.com

First published in Great Britain in 2017 by Weidenfeld &
Nicolson, an imprint of The Orion Publishing Group Ltd.

Library of Congress Cataloging-in-Publication Data

Names: Kisin, Evgeniĭ, 1971– author. | Arshinova, Marina,
editor. | McMillin, Arnold B. (Arnold Barrett), 1941– translator.

Title: Memoirs and reflections / Evgeny Kissin; compiled and
edited by Marina Arshinova; translated by Arnold McMillin.

Description: Lebanon, NH: ForeEdge, 2017.

Identifiers: LCCN 2017040714 (print) | LCCN 2017041725
(ebook) | ISBN 9781512602616 (epub, mobi, & pdf) |
ISBN 9781512602609 (cloth)

Subjects: LCSH: Kisin, Evgeniĭ, 1971– author. |
Pianists—Biography.

Classification: LCC ML417.K664 (ebook) |
LCC ML417.K664 A3 2017 (print) | DDC 786.2092 [B]—dc23

LC record available at https://lccn.loc.gov/2017040714

5 4 3 2 1

I dedicate this book to the blessed memory
of my father.

Contents

Illustrations follow page 94

Preface

June 2014, Paris.

During my life I have had to give many different interviews, and in these interviews I have often been asked – and continue to be asked – the same questions. This book is an attempt to answer all these questions, and at the same time tell of many other things that readers may find interesting: after all, I am in my fifth decade, and have had a great deal of luck; my life has turned out to be extremely full and interesting, so that I have much to recall and relate.

I have just read through the final version of the book and realised that the book is not only and, indeed, not so much about me as about many other people! About the many outstanding and simply good, famous and unknown people whom fate has allowed me to encounter on my life's path. Mixing with them has made my life better, brighter and richer. I am happy and grateful to destiny that all these people have become part of my life and hope that my memoirs will repay the debt. Unfortunately, to mention all the remarkable people whom I have known and still know, it would be necessary to relate my whole life in detail, which, alas, is not possible within the limits of this narrative. I very much hope, therefore, that I shall not offend those friends and acquaintances whose names are not mentioned on the pages of this book.

Evgeny Kissin

'One day, walking on a path from the road to the sea, I saw a boy racing towards me on a bicycle; he was either an adolescent or a teenager . . . Neither word is adequate. For some reason, from the first moment it became clear that rushing towards me was some fantastic Being, living beyond the bounds of any words, definitions or categories, ages and so on. This was a Being of amazing beauty, as if from the canvas of a great Renaissance painter, or from prehistory, when people still resembled gods. Under an immense shock of black curls shone inspired eyes like lanterns in the frame of the fine features of his gentle but already manly face. His strong body, full of unbelievable energy, seemed to be striving to fly – the pedals of a rather miserable little bike seemed ready to sail into the sky . . .

The Being raced past me twice, there and back, and disappeared. I was overwhelmed.'

Vladimir Levi, writer and psychologist. From his reminiscences of Evgeny Kissin.

Part I

CHILDHOOD

My Origin

Scientists continue to discuss the question of nature or nurture on the formation of personality, and it is not for me to judge, but I was definitely lucky in both. Once, a few years ago, one of my listeners expressed her perplexity on the Internet: why, she said, do you, an outstanding musician, publicly express your opinions on political questions such as the elections in Russia and the Arab-Israeli conflict? It is not, she said, 'a matter for tsars'; 'you, Mozart, are unworthy of yourself', quoting Pushkin. Now I shall take the opportunity to explain, in case anybody else is perplexed about this. As for Russia, it is not a matter of indifference to me what is happening in the country in which I was born and became what I am, and where many old friends live. It is a question of upbringing. As for Israel, I was born a Jew and only later became a musician, and all my so-called natural talents come from numerous generations of my ancestors, from my people, and therefore when my people suffer hurt, I consider myself obliged to defend them. It is in my genes.

To tsars I have no, not even the most remote, relationship: my granny and grandad on the paternal side were from Gomel, and on the maternal side from Jewish shtetls in Ukraine and Belarus. My mother worked for many years as a teacher in a district music school, and my father was an engineer. On the whole, 'tsars' have nothing to do with us.

Father

My father was a very kind, sensitive and responsible man who easily made friends, all of whom loved him. All his life he performed daily exercises, and in his youth even boxed. For two years he had served in the army on the Mongolian frontier, where the climate, as is well known, is continental: in summer +40 degrees, in winter -40 degrees. During his military service Father also performed the duties of an artist, drawing and sketching. He had a talent for this, and many years later he made a poster for my first solo recital at our school. Later, over several years before I reached the age of sixteen, he performed a ritual: before each of my performances Father drew, to wish me good luck, a picture of a cat sitting at a piano (after all we are Kissins!),* on the music stand of which were written the names of the composers whose music I was going to play. Father, all his life right up to his death, kept a diary of my concerts, writing very carefully what, when, where and with whom I played.

---

* *Kis* or *Kiska* are Russian affectionate names for cats.

4

In his youth Father was an amateur accordionist, and on a high shelf in our Moscow flat his old accordion is still preserved. For three years he attended evening classes at a music school. All his life Father loved music very much, and on the first anniversary of meeting my mother he gave her the music of Chopin's mazurkas. Father had an excellent ear: after once hearing on the radio or at a concert the voice of an unknown singer, he could infallibly recognise it later.

One morning, a few hours before a heart attack from which he died two days later, the seventy-seven-year-old performed his daily morning exercises. In my childhood Father also showed me how to take exercise, we fenced with plastic swords, we played ball. And Father taught me to play chess. I became very keen on chess, and my parents began to buy me books about it.

When I was born, Father was already thirty-seven. All his life he had dreamed of having a son, and he waited impatiently for my mother to come home from the maternity hospital. On the doors of the eight-metre room in which I subsequently spent my childhood was a bold poster: 'A prince's mansion. Quiet! Quiet! Quiet!'

Mother

I cannot fail to write this section, but it is unbelievably difficult for me to do it. . . It is difficult to speak, especially publicly, about what is most dear and intensely private. What, after all, can be dearer to a person than his own mother, and more private than his relationship with the woman who has in painful birth-pangs given him life?

My mother not only gave life to my sister and me. And not only dedicated all her life to Allochka and me. All Mother's life, her every thought and action has been concentrated on us, on making everything good for us in every way. And she simply cannot do anything else.

Say what you will, but nothing can break the spiritual umbilical cord linking a mother with her children. Therefore, however much Mother and I try to convince each other, we ourselves fully understand that when we have to fly far away from each other, one of us cannot lie down in bed and sleep before the other has rung to say that they have landed safely. And how many times has it gone like this between us:

'How did you sleep?'

'You know, badly last night . . . And you?'

'I could not either.'

This sometimes even frightened my mother, but I think: how very good it is that there are such things in life!

For several decades my mother taught successfully in a music school and was even head of the piano department. Now I hear from various people what a remarkable teacher she was. And all the same, regardless of this, I am convinced that her true calling was precisely to be a mother. If you could see the reactions to her from children of various peoples and races when she looks at them: children, even the tiniest who cannot yet speak, feel it without fail! And when someone else's child is crying in its mother's arms, and my mother makes contact with it from a distance and begins to do something (I cannot even describe what exactly) to calm it – the child becomes calm! And whenever mother and I see little children, say in the park, on public transport or in an airport, my mother will unfailingly every time comment (naturally, her commentaries were only heard by me) on whether the parents before us were behaving towards their child in a way that she considered correct or not. And when I tell my mother about some of my acquaintances whose mothers behaved or behave badly towards them, she is simply incapable of understanding how such a thing is possible.

And yet another characteristic feature of my mother: taking care of all the members of our family. She pays no attention to herself, she is simply unable to do so. But when we try to persuade her to look after herself, she only becomes annoyed.

For many years of my childhood, Mother, although she never taught me music in the direct sense of the word, sat with me at the piano every day for hours while I practised, watching to make sure that I did everything as it should be done. Musical pedagogues know well how important this is, and without many years of help

I should not have become what I became. And later, for many years, Mother would come to my piano lessons, and my teacher Anna Pavlovna Kantor would regularly ask her opinion and always listen carefully to it, even if they differed somewhat. When we moved to the West, Mother, together with Anna Pavlovna, began to conduct my affairs, to co-ordinate my timetable and negotiate with my impresarios on all matters. At first I could not care less about all these practical issues; I just wanted to play the piano, and remain untouched by organisational questions; years passed before I learned to deal with all this myself. And Mother always did everything possible to protect me from all practical and other cares and worries, so that I could peacefully work and devote myself to art. Truly she has dedicated her whole life to concern for me. To the present day Mother is nervous during my concerts, sometimes even more than I. And when she sees that I am very anxious, she embraces me, squeezing me tightly, and says: 'Give it away, give to me your anxiety!' Oh, if only she had more often allowed us to look after her . . . and I hope she lives for many more years . . .

Grandma and Grandpa

I do not remember Grandpa Boris, my father's father: he died when I had not yet reached the age of three. I do recall Grandma Manya, Father's mother, but I did not see much of her. In childhood, however, I spent a lot of time with my mother's parents, Grandpa Arkady (Aron) and Grandma Rakhil, mainly in summer at the dacha. Grandpa Arkady worked his whole life at a car plant that during World War II produced tanks, so that, unlike Grandpa Boris who was on active service for the whole war, he did not have to fight: his factory and all its workers were evacuated to the village of Vyry on the Volga. Grandpa and Grandma, with my then four-year-old mother, were settled amongst the local people, and once the landlady asked Grandma:

'You know they say that in your Moscow there live Jews?'

'Yes,' replied Grandma.

'And what are they like?'

'Well, we here are Jews,' said Grandma, and heard in response:

'But you are humans! So who are those Jews then?'

Grandma worked as a bookkeeper. I know no details, for in my childhood it never occurred to me to question her about it – and she died when I was sixteen. To this day I regret that I never had the chance to speak to her as one grown-up to another – and I am very glad that with Grandpa, who outlived Grandma by eleven months and lived with us for several months before his death, I had that experience. And how very important that was . . . As with Mother and Father, nobody can replace Grandma and Grandpa. For that reason I cannot help envying those people who lost their grandparents less early, and had time to communicate with them in adulthood.

At the time Grandma died, Grandpa was in hospital. He was in a very serious condition after an operation and the doctors did not expect him to survive, but prescribed for him a double course of some antibiotic medicine that affected the aural nerve, so poor Grandpa became completely deaf. After a while we took Grandpa home, and it was at that time that I communicated with him extensively. But he could hear nothing and I therefore wrote to him and he replied in speech. At that time Grandpa managed to tell me about many things before he was again taken to hospital, from which that time he did not return.

For example, he told me that he had a first cousin once removed, Abram Ananyevich Kissin, who in the 1920s and 1930s had been head of the Organisation for Corn Exports, but who was arrested at the end of the 1930s and exiled to Astrakhan. We discussed this in autumn 1988; at that time it was no longer dangerous for people to speak about such things. Grandpa's story remained with me for several years after that, and I recalled it under particular circumstances which had the most unexpected and remarkable consequences for all our family – more about this later.

Here I should say that Kissin is the name of my mother; Father's name was Otman, and several years before I was born, when Allochka was preparing to enter the Central Music School, her teacher, Anna Danilovna Artobolevskaya, invited Father for an interview in which she said that with such a Jewish surname Allochka, for all her excellent musical ability, would not be allowed to enter the school, and so Father had to take Mother's name, which sounds more Russian, and I have borne it since birth.

How my grandpa adored me . . . In early childhood I read in some book that flies were highly infectious, spreading many terrible diseases. I remember that at the end of that paragraph there was the following statement: 'Together with salted fish and cheese, the sulphuric fly penetrates human intestines and chews them until the person dies.' This made such an impression on me that I began to fall into a panic at the sight of flies, and at the dacha when I was eating Grandpa would stand beside me with a towel and drive them away. Also at the dacha Grandpa taught me to ride a bicycle and at first ran behind me down the street, fearing that I might fall. And my grandma also adored me, of course. She would call me 'the dearest person in the world and in his grandma's life'.

They were good-hearted, honest, modest, decent, wise people. Nowadays I recall how when I was small Grandpa would always repeat the word 'discipline', and I understand how right he was, how this very discipline is important, indeed essential, in life, and particularly in the life of an artist. And my mother often recalls various sayings of my grandma, simple and wise. For instance, how one should not cross the road in front of a moving vehicle: 'Don't make the driver nervous – he is also a person.' Or the advice that Grandma would give my mother: 'It is better for you to have one very good dress than several bad ones: what is expensive is pleasant, what is cheap decays.' When, aged six, my sister Allochka returned from hospital after having her appendix out and began to sing popular songs she had heard in hospital containing swear words, naturally not understanding anything, Mother was horrified, but Grandma said: 'Pay no attention to it and she will soon forget it all,' as indeed happened. And when I was small and my mother tried to instil something in me and I did not listen, wise Grandma said: 'It is not sinking in. When he grows up he will understand.'

I think my musical genes come not only from my parents, but also from Grandma and Grandpa. My grandma loved singing, and sang Jewish and Russian songs with exceptional purity and musicality; she always sang while doing housework, and when Allochka and I were small she sang us cradle songs. Grandpa had a small mandolin on which he played absolutely everything by ear, and one day, visiting his sister, he took in his hands (for the first time in his life) her son's violin, and, after moving the bow slightly over the strings, began to play. Grandma and Grandpa were not religious, but they observed certain Jewish traditions: not so long ago my mother told me that they fasted at Yom Kippur and on some Jewish holidays went to the synagogue, and bought mat-zoth at Passover. And when Allochka asked Grandma whether she believed in G-d, Grandma replied thus: 'In ancient times there were wise people.'

My Sister Allochka

When Mummy informed ten-year-old Allochka that soon she would have a little brother or sister, she said in reply, 'What were you thinking about earlier? Now it won't be interesting for him with me or for me with him.' Things, however, turned out quite differently. Allochka waited eagerly for the appearance of a new member of the family and went with my father and grandmother to the maternity hospital to collect Mummy and me. Seeing me, she exclaimed, 'Whoever is born on a Sunday is simply a beauty' – and from that very early period of my life all members of my family continued to call me 'beauty' (and I really was born on that day of the week). Later on, Allochka always helped my mother and father to look after me: to feed, wash and dress me, and play with me. When I was about one year old Allochka wrote an essay about me, and her teacher of Russian said to Mummy that far from all mothers could write so touchingly and with such understanding and love about their child.

Allochka studied piano at the Central Music School and was very talented. When my future teacher, Anna Pavlovna Kantor, said to her teacher, Tatyana Evgenevna Kestner, with whom she was studying in the CMS, that they had brought her the younger brother of Alla Kissina, the latter said to her, 'If he is even half as talented as his sister, take him without hesitation; she is one of the best pupils in the school.' Allochka played me everything that I requested, and when I myself began to play the piano, we performed many duets together. We studied in different schools, and when I entered the Gnessin Ten-year School Allochka was already quite grown-up and we each had different interests and occupations.

For ten years, until we left Russia, Alla worked as an accompanist in the same children's music school no. 38 (it is now named after Emil Gilels) as where our mother worked. In the West she had no permanent work, as we frequently moved from one country to another, but from time to time Alla resumed her work as an accompanist.

All her life, from early childhood, Allochka had a great thirst for knowledge, and in her childhood they called her 'a bag full of questions'. When, during Allochka's school years, Mummy attempted to help her with her homework by making suggestions, she would say, 'I shall not write that: it was not my head that thought of it!' Now she possesses an immense quantity of knowledge of the widest range of subjects, from aesthetic theory to astrology.

Allochka is a very kind and sensitive person; she always tries to help everyone so far as her ability and circumstances allow. When my mother and I are not at home, she most devotedly and solicitously looks after Anna Pavlovna, helping her in everything. All our acquaintances and friends are extremely fond of my sister.

Zhenechka, There Is a Piano There!

My parents used to say that at eleven months I first sang by ear: the theme of the A major Fugue from the second book of Bach's *Well-Tempered Clavier* in the keys of the tonic and dominant,* which Allochka was then studying. From that time I began to sing everything that I heard around me: on the radio, on records, the repertoires of Allochka and my mother's pupils who came to us for lessons. When Allochka was sitting at the piano I often sat on her knees, sang, and demanded that she play what I was singing, but when she played from the music I remembered it and later always turned over the pages for her. When I began to walk, every morning on waking I would run to the piano and demand, 'O'en it, o'en it, o'en the wid!' And when I was two years and

---

* The key of the tonic is the basic key of a work. The key of the dominant is opposite to the key of the tonic.

two months old I myself began to play on the piano everything I heard around me. At about this time the factory where my father worked allotted, to improve living conditions, a separate flat in which Grandma and Grandpa settled. Up to then the six of us lived in a thirty-six-metre three-room flat, and when I first went to Grandma's new flat I walked and looked around, then asked:

'And where's the piano?'

They replied:

'There is no piano here.'

'How, no piano?'

I was sincerely amazed. In that year they brought me to the house of friends for the birthday of their daughter, who is now my wife. Our hosts opened the door and I, alarmed by the noise and the profusion of unfamiliar faces, took a step back and refused to go in. Then my mother whispered in my ear, 'Zhenechka, but there is a piano!', and I like a lunatic went in the direction indicated by my mother, sat at the piano – and didn't leave it all evening. And that, in my mother's words, is how my childhood was.

One of my earliest memories was of sitting at our old Bechstein (by that time my parents had bought a grand piano), and playing by ear, improvising, composing a song about how our neighbour at the dacha treated their dog called Gypsy badly, and my father recorded me on his old Adidas tape recorder with large brown bobbins. On the music stand hung an ivory-coloured microphone the size of the palm of a hand. Then Father wound the tape back and I heard how I had been trying to sing the popular Soviet song 'A Strange Star Shines' in a low voice and Father said to me, 'You sang this the day before yesterday.'

I have often been asked whether I was deprived of my childhood in starting to play the piano so early. Absolutely not! I had a normal childhood, nobody ever forced me to play the piano, I spent a lot of time in the street with other children, and altogether did everything I wanted. And I very much liked being naughty in childhood. But the point is that, more than anything else in the world, from early childhood I wanted nothing more than to play the piano, picking up music by heart and improvising to my heart's content.

The Beginning

My first public performance was when I was in the first class, and at a school concert in the hall of our Gnessin Ten-year School I played the C major Variations by Haydn, and afterwards asked what mark I had been given. At that time I did not know the difference between a concert and an exam.

Beyond the school, I first performed in the Railwaymen's House of Culture; again the concert was given by Gnessin pupils. At that concert I played four of my own compositions; on the poster stood out vividly, 'Kissin, 4 Pieces. Performed by the composer.' After my performance, passing along the row to my place in the hall, I heard a male voice say: 'That's him, the composer.'

My first performance with an orchestra – that was an interesting story. When I was in the third year, at the end of the school year Boris Iosifovich Kaprov, the director of the orchestra of the youngest classes at our school and my great admirer, said to Anna Pavlovna, 'In September there will be a competition in the school for the best performance of the first movement of Bach's D minor Concerto with our orchestra. Let Zhenya learn it. The winner of the competition will play in the Great Hall of the Gnessin Institute.' Anna Pavlovna gave me Bach's concerto to study over the summer, which I did, but by September she had forgotten about the competition, and when at the beginning of the school year I played her the piece she said, 'Fine, put it aside for the time being, we'll study some other things first.' Sometime later Boris Iosifovich asked Anna Pavlovna, 'Why is Zhenya not coming to rehearsals? All the other children are already rehearsing with the orchestra.' This conversation took place on Saturday, and the competition was to be on Wednesday of the following week; then Anna Pavlovna rang my mother, explaining the situation and requesting that I prepare the first movement of the concerto by Monday.

On Monday I again played Anna Pavlovna the first

movement, and on Wednesday went to school early as Boris Iosifovich said that, because I had attended no rehearsals with the orchestra, before the beginning of the competition we should at least play together once. I had no idea how one should play with an orchestra and paid no attention to the orchestra, so nothing came together. At that moment the director of our school, Zinovy Isaakovich Finkelstein (nicknamed ZIF) came into the hall, and, having heard our 'ensemble', remarked, 'Well, he's still small.' Boris Iosifovich, however, believed in me and asked, 'Let him play, it is after all only a school competition.' Lots were drawn, and I got the first ticket. Anna Pavlovna understood that this was no good, as I had to listen first to how the others played; then she asked a girl from the top form who had got the last ticket whether she would swap tickets with me, and the girl agreed gladly as she was happy to get it over early. And so the competition begins, everybody plays, Anna Pavlovna and I sit together with an open score and listen. Anna Pavlovna points out to me all the mistakes in the other children's performances, and explains that I should pay attention as to how one should play with an orchestra. Finally my turn comes and I play and, the youngest of the competitors, am unanimously awarded first prize! Later we even recorded this movement for the radio, and to this day I still have the cassette with that recording: well, for a ten-year-old it is not bad at all.

And a few months later I first played a whole concerto. This took place in Ulyanovsk; with the local orchestra conducted by Evgeny Tsirlin I played Mozart's Piano Concerto in D minor. I remember that in a review were the words, 'We must hope that a great future awaits Zhenya as a performing musician.'

My First Solo Recital

My very first solo recital took place in May 1983 in the hall of our school. In the first half I played the D minor Concerto by Bach-Marcello, the F minor Prelude and Fugue by Mendelssohn, some Chopin mazurkas, Liszt's étude 'Forest Murmurs' and Schumann's Abegg Variations; the second half featured Chopin's Second Piano Concerto with, on a second piano, a former pupil of Anna Pavlovna, Elena Petrovna Ivanova, who is now one of the leading teachers of piano in our school. During the interval I could not wait for the start of the second half and kept asking, 'Well, when will they ring the bell?' – I was so eager to get back onto the platform. Very many people came to the recital (our director Zinovy Isaakovich, I remember, had to stand behind the platform because there was no seat for him in the hall, and Anna Pavlovna stood rather than sat). It was a great success, and after the concert, still standing in the hall, an old friend of Anna Pavlovna, Lyudmila Nikolayevna Lukovnikova, whose husband was at that time director of the House of Composers, said to Anna Pavlovna, 'Andrey should arrange a recital for him in the House of Composers!'

'No, he shouldn't, Lucia,' objected Anna Pavlovna, 'He's still small and we shouldn't overburden him with concerts.'

Suddenly a man who had come with Lyudmila Nikolayevna entered the conversation.

'Forgive me, please, for intruding, but I should like to say something to you. I am a doctor; not a paediatrician, but a doctor. You are absolutely right that a child of that age should not be overburdened with concerts. But when I noticed a few minutes ago the enthusiasm with which Zhenya came out every time to play encores, I understood that still more terrible for him would be to "burn out". It is clear that you love him, and you will feel how many concerts he needs.'

Anna Pavlovna was convinced by his arguments, and a month and a half later I repeated the same programme, only adding to 'Forest Murmurs' another Liszt étude that I had learned in the meantime, 'La leggierezza', in the House of Composers. The hall only had 600 seats and tickets were distributed free, so many more people came than there were places for in the hall. Chairs were set up over all the platform, and Mother stood off-stage. When, after the recital, Anna Pavlovna asked me whether the people sitting alongside me on the platform had been a distraction, I without hesitation said what I felt: 'They helped me!'

And so it has been with me my whole life: I have always loved to play for people. And the larger the audience in the hall, the more inspired I feel. But once, many years ago, I first played in Montreal, where at that time I was unknown. Before the recital they told me that not all the tickets had been sold, and I, very disappointed, started to complain that I should not be inspired, and a man, far from music, who was looking after me uttered a phrase that I have remembered all my life: 'You should not punish those who came for those who did not.'

Sharing What Is Precious

Many years later, when I was already living in the West, certain journalists started to ask me the question, 'Who could you have become if you were not a musician?' At first I did not know how to reply, because it had never crossed my mind. But this question, put to me for the twentieth time, started to interest me and I began to reflect: if, let us say, I did not have a musical talent, then who would I like to be? And I came to the conclusion that, in that case, I would like to be a tour guide or an independent journalist. And a bit later still I understood why: these professions, musical performer, tour guide and independent journalist, have something in common – all three share with other people what they love, what is to them dear, important and interesting. And then at last I understood why in childhood I had so liked playing for people, and why the more people came to my concerts, the more it inspired me: I had a natural, unconscious and very strong desire to share with others what I loved more than anything else in the world, what for me was the most important and dear thing in life.

For the same reason, of course, from early childhood I loved reciting – after all, readers and declaimers also share with the public what they love; it seems to me that in general it is the closest profession to that of a performing musician, and we musicians as well as readers and actors perform works created by other people. Preserved on a high shelf in our Moscow flat there are still magnetic tapes which recorded how I, at the age of three, recited in various appropriate voices Tolstoy's 'Three Bears' and poems by Mikhalkov. As a teenager I liked to recite Blok, Voloshin, Mayakovsky, Sasha Chorny, Bagritsky, Utkin, Zoshchenko, Ilf and Petrov . . . and later Galich. And in recent years, at the request of various people, I sometimes give poetic evenings, reading poems in Russian and Yiddish. One such evening was held with Gérard Depardieu: I read Russian and Jewish poems in the original, and he read literal prose translations in French.

This is how it came about. After one of my recitals, which Depardieu attended, he proposed that we perform together. Naturally I was very embarrassed and began to decline, but he insisted; then I asked, 'Maybe, in that case, you will teach me how to do this professionally?'

To which Depardieu replied jokingly: 'There is nothing to teach you: from the way you announced your encores to the public, I understood that you can do it very well.'

And a few years later a joint poetic evening was held in the beautiful old town of Montpellier in the south of France, as part of its summer festival. And later I even recorded three compact discs of Jewish poetry; it is interesting that the greatest number of sales of these discs was to Japan!

But of course I always emphasise, so that everyone understands and there is not the least doubt about it: my profession is playing the piano, and verse-reading is only a hobby. And, as a rule, I do not recite for the public but for a narrow circle of friends, often even for individuals whom I wish to acquaint with a work of literature or non-fiction that I like. For example, I much enjoy reciting Voinovich's *A Portrait Against the Background of a Myth*, which I have nearly learned entirely by heart. Or extracts from Ilya Gililov's *The Shakespeare Game: The Mystery of the Great Phoenix* (in the 1990s this was a bestseller in Russia). Or the articles of Vladimir Jabotinsky. And in English I absolutely love to read aloud an excellent, epoch-making article called 'Two cheers for colonialism', written a decade ago by the Indian-born American political scientist Dinesh D'Souza, in which the author demonstrates independence of thought and a deep knowledge of history, including that of science and economics, and quite brilliantly debunks, one after the other, the Marxist myths, widespread in the last century, that the West grew rich at the expense of the colonies it had robbed, and that without Western imperialism those Third World countries would, supposedly, have developed more rapidly and the people there would have had better lives. Stone by stone D'Souza demolishes all these stereotypes, which have eaten into the consciousness and even sub-consciousness of many devotees of left-wing political correctness.

It is possible that my love of reciting comes from Grandpa Arkady: he too very much loved to read aloud newspaper articles to members of the family. And I sometimes like to recite poetry, prose or articles when I am on my own; for example, standing in the shower (they say many people like to sing, but I personally like to recite!), or when on tour and there are a few free minutes in a hotel room – it helps me to relax. Because for us musicians, relaxing, particularly when on tour, is extremely necessary – and that is the method I have found for myself.

My First Radio Broadcast

In 1983, a significant year, as I have already mentioned, the overseas broadcasting channel made a programme about me in English. I recorded for this broadcast seven pieces, including Schumann's Abegg Variations, and they conducted an interview with Anna Pavlovna and me. Later there were many responses to this broadcast from around the world. I shall quote from memory a few of the more amusing ones. One of the listeners, I think from Japan, did not believe that an eleven-year-old boy could play in that way and asked, 'Perhaps Anna Kantor herself was playing?' A listener from Chicago wrote, 'I can imagine how many thousands Evgeny earns for a recital. He, as you told us, is also recording for the radio and gramophone records. Soon he, a child, will be a millionaire, remember my words. And it is right: such a talented person who also knows how to work like an ox should be a millionaire.'

And here is a letter from Ireland of a quite different nature. Its author, clearly a Communist, wrote: 'Of course such a wunderkind could be born in any country of the world. But the fine attention that he receives can only be given in your country. Just think, free teaching in a music school! Where else is that possible?'

A listener from Poland requested, 'Tell me please when Kissin's next recitals will be in Poland or the

DDR, I can also come to a recital by him in Berlin.' I remember how my mother laughed: 'He can but we cannot.' At that time we did not even dream of travel abroad.

A listener from Finland was more abrupt: 'I trust you will not hide him behind your "iron curtain", but will show him in Europe or America?'

And finally, this is what interested a female listener in Sweden: 'Please describe the house where Evgeny Kissin lives, his rooms, study, bedroom and nursery. Describe what he is given for breakfast, lunch and dinner, what dishes he prefers, what colour he likes best.' I remind you that with my parents and sister we lived in a thirty-six-metre three-bedroom flat.

Debuts in Leningrad and Moscow

After my first solo recitals, in November 1983 I played twice, for the first time, the whole of Chopin's Second Piano Concerto. It was in the magnificent Great Hall of the Leningrad Philharmonia with its Symphony Orchestra under the Yugoslav conductor Nikolaj Žličar. After that, I learned Chopin's First Piano Concerto and played it for the first time in February 1984 in Sverdlovsk with the orchestra of the Sverdlovsk Philharmonia under a very good conductor and pleasant man, Andrey Chistiakov. And on 27 March 1984 I performed my debut in the Great Hall of the Moscow Conservatoire, which later became my favourite hall throughout my life; I played Chopin's two concertos with the Moscow Philharmonic Orchestra under Dmitry Kitayenko. At that time the violinist Vadim Repin, my contemporary, was already performing brilliantly, and after I grew to be famous we became, as it were, joint 'leading wunderkinds of the USSR'; a little later Maxim Vengerov joined us in that status.

When I am asked about the influence of wunderkind status on me, I always reply honestly that such things interested me less than anything else in the world; this will be verified by anyone who knew me at that time. On the other hand, in those years my parents and Anna Pavlovna never missed the least opportunity to criticise me, and after my successful performances, when there were no particular reasons for criticism, they always said to me that now people would be expecting still more of me and that I should fulfil these expectations. I learned early on in life the expression, 'The more you give, the more will be asked of you.'

And one more thing: I remember that then many musicians, particularly the prominent Russian pianist and teacher Dmitry Aleksandrovich Bashkirov, would publicly say that the category of wunderkind did not apply to me, because by that word people usually meant striking technical achievements, whereas in my playing at that time they noted a particular musicality, maturity and depth.

Tikhon Nikolayevich Khrennikov

In 1984 the director of our school, Zinovy Isaakovich Finkelstein, decided that it would be a good idea to show me to Tikhon Nikolayevich Khrennikov. We agreed to meet on 1 May and Anna Pavlovna and I set off to Khrennikov's home. Our host welcomed us warmly, leading us into his study where there were already many people: the wife of Tikhon Nikolayevich, Klara Arnoldovna, their daughter Natalia with her husband, the director of our school, Zinovy Isaakovich, the composers Lev Solin and Aleksandr Tchaikovsky, the latter with his then wife Irina Vinogradova, and others.

That day I played many things for Tikhon Nikolayevich and the other people present, including some of my own compositions (in childhood I did a lot of composing). I had prepared thoroughly for this meeting, and played well. Tikhon Nikolayevich was very satisfied, saying, 'I am ready to listen until morning!', and he invited me to participate in the Second International Festival of Contemporary Music, which was to take place in Moscow under his direction only a few weeks later. On the 23rd, with Vadim Repin, whom Khrennikov was actively supporting at that time, I played a recital under the aegis of this festival in the Small Hall of the Moscow Conservatoire: I performed in the first half, Vadim in the second.

Tikhon Nikolayevich also took part in the festival

as a soloist, playing in the Great Hall of the Moscow Conservatoire his Third Piano Concerto. Then after the concert I went to Khrennikov in the green room, and he gave me a book by L. Grigoryev and Y. Platek about himself, *Khrennikov: His Life and Time*, writing on the title page, 'To Zhenechka Kissin with admiration, Tikhon Khrennikov'.

At our first meeting on 1 May 1984, Tikhon Nikolayevich asked Anna Pavlovna why I was so pale. Anna Pavlovna explained that I got very tired because we lived a long way from my school, and I was spending much time and strength on the journey. Tikhon Nikolayevich immediately made a note, 'Bring him closer,' and in June the following year, thanks to his efforts, we received authorisation to occupy a new flat only half an hour from the Gnessin School. This flat is ours to this very day. Moving there, my parents were obliged to sell our old Bechstein, as it would not go in the lift, and to carry it up a narrow staircase to the fourteenth (in reality the seventeenth) floor was, of course, impossible. Thus I was left practically without an instrument, as an upright piano was no use to me for practising by then, and once again, thanks to Tikhon Nikolayevich, the State Music Fund allowed me the use of grand pianos free of charge. Right up to my departure from the USSR at the end of 1991 I practised on an 'Estonia' piano belonging to the Music Fund. At that time, during our first meeting, Tikhon Nikolayevich considered that 'pale Zhenechka Kissin' needed not only to avoid wasting his strength on trolleybuses and the underground travelling to school, but should also relax under good conditions, and from that time, thanks to him, every summer and every winter until our departure from the country we spent our holidays in Homes for Composers in the countryside, especially 'Ruza'. What a time that was, what an atmosphere, what conversations in those unforgettable Homes! How I should like to spend another vacation in that same 'Ruza'! But, as I have been told recently by old friends who had been there, almost nothing remains of that 'Ruza' now, alas.

That is the sort of man he was. Later I learned, and even now continue to learn, that I was just one of the large number of people who were helped by Khrennikov. What is more, unlike many others, Tikhon Nikolayevich was not at all inclined to speak, especially publicly, about his numerous good deeds.

In later years we kept in close touch. In the summer of 1986 I learned his Second Piano Concerto and played it in various cities and countries. Together with Tikhon Nikolayevich, Vadim Repin and Maxim Vengerov I played at the Schleswig-Holstein Festival, and in Odessa and Moscow at 'Khrennikov's Creative Evenings'. First Maxim played the Second Violin Concerto; then Tikhon Nikolayevich himself played his own Third Piano Concerto, and after the interval I performed his

Second Piano Concerto and Vadim finished the programme with his First Violin Concerto. Those were
merry journeys!

Every year Anna Pavlovna, my mother and I, if at
that time we were in Moscow, would visit Tikhon
Nikolayevich on his birthday. The Khrennikovs' house
was one of the most hospitable homes that I have visited in my life, and I have been in many – in various
countries, on various continents. In those days Tikhon
Khrennikov's huge flat was always full of people: to it
would come his many friends, colleagues, pupils . . .
And unfailingly the atmosphere was one of warmth,
cordiality, goodness and love.

Nowadays when I meet with my friends we like to
sing the songs of our past (as a rule I am the accompanist on such occasions). And we definitely always sing a
song loved by millions of people of several generations:
'Moscow Windows'. I think that even if Khrennikov had
written nothing except this wonderful song, his name
would still have gone down in history. We remember
it and sing: 'It has been dear to me for many years, and
there is nothing brighter than it, the undying light of
Moscow windows . . .'

Blessed memory to you, dear Tikhon Nikolayevich!

I Have Been Lucky to Meet Good People in My Life

From early childhood I have met many good people who have helped me a great deal. These were not only my family and Anna Pavlovna, but the administrators and teaching staff of the Gnessin School and the Gnessin Institute. Thanks to them, and despite the school rules, I was able to attend far less often than the other children and had various other privileges, allowing me to devote as much time as I liked to music. There was also Vladimir Teodorovich Spivakov, who shortly after my debut with the two Chopin concertos began constantly to invite me as a soloist with his remarkable orchestra 'Moscow Virtuosi'. When the authorities did not want me to travel abroad, it was Spivakov who managed to arrange for me to go with the 'Virtuosi' on a tour in Hungary. When the friend and long-standing partner of Spivakov, Boris Bekhterev, decided to leave the Soviet Union, Vladimir Teodorovich bought from him a small Steinway grand piano and gave it to me as a present. It was very old and frail, but in those years, as is common with many adolescent male pianists, I loved to 'hammer' and for that reason was constantly breaking strings; but to get Steinway strings in the Soviet Union was, as anyone can imagine, absolutely impossible, at any rate for our family at that particular moment, so I had to preserve Spivakov's present and practise, as I said earlier, on the 'Estonia' of the Music Fund.

In the mid-1980s Anna Pavlovna received a letter from Leningrad written by a woman she did not know called Izabella Abramovna Gutkina. The writer said she was a musician, a teacher of cello and a big fan of mine; that she was very ill and did not have long to live, and that she would very much like to help our family. Mother, being a proud woman, categorically refused, regardless of our modest material situation at that time. But when, during one of our regular journeys to Leningrad, we became acquainted with this remarkable person, my mother understood that she should not refuse this help. Soon after, Izabella Abramovna died, and bequeathed to me her audio library.

Immense thanks and a deep bow to all these people!

Vagram Saradjian

I first met this talented cellist and very pleasant, warm man in July 1987 at a festival in Tours, France, where many Soviet musicians performed regularly. It turned out that a month later our family and Vagram, with his wife and son, were vacationing in the Composers' Home in Jūrmala, and there we really got to know each other and became close.

I was at the age when adolescents seek models to imitate in male adults, and want to resemble some of them. I liked Vagram greatly: tall, handsome, noisy, merry, witty and unbelievably sociable. He was a normal anti-Soviet member of the intelligentsia of his time; I recall how he would tell an anecdote in which a soloist exclaims, quoting a poem by Yevtushenko, 'Do the Russians want war?!', and the choir quietly joins in rhythmically, 'They do, they do, they do, they do!' We formed a close relationship and on returning to Moscow started seeing each other frequently; it turned out that we lived not far from each other. It was Vagram who acquainted me with masterpieces from the cello repertoire. We made much music together and once even gave a concert in our school: Beethoven's Variations on a Theme of Mozart, Schumann's Three Fantasy Pieces, Falla's *Pièces Espagnoles* and Shostakovich's Cello Sonata; for encores we played Rachmaninov's *Vocalise* and Shchedrin's *Quadrille*. After my concerts in Moscow it was Vagram who drove my family and me home, as at that time we did not own a car.

At the Moscow Conservatoire Vagram had in his time studied with Rostropovich, and when we had got to know each other he told me many remarkable stories about him. I cannot resist repeating some of them.

A student of Rostropovich, the future famous cellist Karine Georgian, whose father was a well-known cello teacher, is playing to Mstislav Leopoldovich Brahms's First Sonata. As always at Rostropovich's classes, the room is full of people. Karine is playing – and

Rostropovich is sitting and from time to time making remarks like the following:

'You are pwaying rewowtingly . . . Your father is an idiot . . . Si'ply a kwetin: he couldn't teach you . . .'

Karine weeps and continues to play, Mstislav Leopoldovich continues to utter remarks like: 'Your father is an idiot!'

– and then suddenly jumps up with a cry: 'What are you sniwelling here for?! What wight have I to tawk abowt your fawther like that? Why din't you jump up and giw me a smawk in the face?! Get out of my class!!'

Once Rostropovich went to an All-Union Cello Competition in which two of his girl students were taking part. One was slightly better than the other, but in the final the worse one took the first prize ahead of the stronger one. Everyone who knew them was very surprised at such a result. Rostropovich explained it thus: 'The day before the last wouwnd, they both played fwigging awfully, and I curwsed them with sewect swear words. One laughed, and the owther one wept. So: the fiwst pwize was won by the one who laughed!'

For many years Rostropovich's accompanist was Aleksandr Dedyukhin, whom Rostropovich used to nickname the 'choirboy'. 'It is not because you sing in a cwire, but because you pway like a fewet, like a fewet,' and demonstrated how Dedyukhin bent low over the keyboard.* All this Rostropovich did in a kind spirit, with love. Later Dedyukhin often accompanied Vagram too, and one day, when Rostropovich had already emigrated to the West, and Vagram and Dedyukhin were on tour in some country and had gone to their hotel rooms, Vagram rang Dedyukhin and began to speak to him in Rostropovich's voice, 'Fewet, how aw you!' Afterwards Dedyukhin told everyone, 'Slava rang me!', and Vagram did not tell him the secret in order not to disappoint him. Dedyukhin was apparently given a hard time by cellists.

Vagram told me quite a bit about his studies with Rostropovich. One day, after he had prepared thoroughly for his lesson, Rostropovich utterly demolished him with criticisms, saying that he had not practised. Vagram took offence, and, upset, did not practise at all, but at the next lesson Rostropovich said to him, 'Now I see that you have been pwactising well! Eweything sounds compweteley diffewent!' I, incidentally, can understand this, because from my own experience I know that the results of work are sometimes not evident immediately but sometime later, when what you have done is put away into your muscle memory.

And one day Rostropovich gave Vagram Chopin's Nocturne in D flat in an arrangement for cello. First he

---

* 'fewet' is an attempt to reproduce Rostropovich's accent for ferret (*khorek* in Russian), while the word for choir (*khor*) is related in sound though not meaning.

told Vagram to learn the nocturne on the piano, and then when Vagram brought the cello arrangement to the lesson and, after the piano introduction, played the first note, Rostropovich said, 'No!' Again the pianist played the short introduction and Vagram played the first note – 'No!' This was repeated about ten times, and Vagram was ready to get up and go when Rostropovich said, 'Evewy instwumentalist, evewy conductor, evewy singer takes the fiwst note only after taking bweath or the upbeat!' And incidentally, said Vagram, 'That was a remarkable lesson!'

Unfortunately Vagram did not manage to make a solo career in America: he came there too late for that, he was already over forty. Now Vagram Georgievich has been teaching for many years at the Houston Music Academy. He is a good man . . . as a wit once observed: Saradzhan – Sara – dzhan – dear Sara.*

My School, Our Ten-year Gnessin

It is one of my brightest and warmest memories of my childhood, of my life in Russia. I did not go to school as frequently as the other children, as at first I was often ill, and then I began to give concerts. Now the building of our school has been repaired and extended; I have not yet seen what has been done inside,

---

* *Dzhan* means 'dear' in Armenian.

but am sad that it will no longer be as I remember it. When I last crossed its threshold on one of my visits to Moscow about ten years ago, some things had been changed and I experienced a feeling of regret. Of course this is inevitable, everything needs repairs and rebuilding, but I am nonetheless melancholy that the school I remember, which will always remain in my memory, in my heart, will never be there any more. But I recall with nostalgia all our classrooms on three floors: the basement where in the preliminary year we studied rhythm and solfeggio, and in the older classes military training, where we simply loved to run at break time, during which G-d alone knows how many lamps I broke (I can talk about it now!); and two recreation rooms, in one of which we in the youngest classes used to play piggyback; and the hall where tests were held, exams, concerts, satirical revues and, on rare occasions, lectures on various topics (on 1 September so-called 'lessons about peace', that is, lectures on the international situation, were given to us by the historian Viktor Yuryevich Dashevsky); and the laboratory in which the extremely kind Lyudmila Valentinovna Kostina taught me physics, and Grigory Borisovich Minkin, nicknamed 'Mushroom',* Russian language and literature. There were niches on either side of the

---

* The first letters of Minkin's name (Gri and B) spell the Russian word for mushroom (*grib*).

entrance to the school, on the walls of which I as a child became acquainted with indecent words, and once I saw inscribed 'Beat the Yids, save Russia!'; and even our dirty lavatories with unforgettable inscriptions on the wall like 'Long live humour and satire on the walls of our *sortir* [bog]!'

Viktor Yuryevich Dashevsky – Teacher of History

Because of my frequent illnesses, and later my early concerts and travels, the director of our school, Zinovy Isaakovich Finkelstein, arranged for me a so-called programme of voluntary attendance, and several teachers of general subjects began to give me one-to-one lessons.

Much time and attention was devoted to me by Viktor Yuryevich Dashevsky, our history teacher. At first he said that I might be musically talented, but was generally a pupil of average ability. Later, however, being in love with history, he was gradually able to arouse my interest in his subject, and one fine day, hearing my reply on the topic 'five features of imperialism', he became greatly enthused and started to say that such a reply should be given as a model to university students. At first our lessons were conducted during walks in the Aleksandrovsky Gardens and on Red Square, thanks to the fact that our school was situated nearby. During our first walk he showed me Pashkov's House, telling me about it and explaining what columns and pediments were; and a few months later he told me (unfortunately his unforgettable intonation cannot be conveyed in written form): 'And now Pashkov's House is in such a state that it may collapse. To be honest, I am very sorry that it has not fallen down already, for if it had done there would have been such a scandal!', and he explained that in *Literaturka** there had just been an article saying that, because of the gross foolishness of those who had planned the recently constructed Borovitskaya metro station directly underneath Pashkov's House, the building was in danger. Another time I remember that Viktor Yuryevich started talking about the above-mentioned inscription in the niche, 'Beat the Yids', and explained that one should not be too upset about it because the people who wrote such things did not mean anything serious but simply, so to speak, joked – as in the film *The Prisoner of the Caucasus*, when he says that if you don't help us, we'll cut your throat, adding 'Joke'. I was surprised: could people really joke like that? Viktor Yuryevich agreed that one really should not.

It must be said that in our family people did not talk about politics in front of the children, and so I was completely ignorant about such things, and Viktor Yuryevich was the first to tell me that 'at the end of the 1940s and beginning of the 1950s there were great

---

* *Literaturnaya gazeta* was a weekly newspaper on literary and social affairs that was popular with the intelligentsia from the 1960s to the 1980s.

injustices committed against the Jews in our country,' and in general that Stalin was 'a bad man'. He always told his pupils this and explained in detail, although, as is well known, before perestroika such talk was not approved.

When our family, thanks to the efforts of Tikhon Nikolayevich Khrennikov, took possession of a new flat and moved from the Varshavsky Highway to Sokolniki, Viktor Yuryevich started to come to us and teach me at our home. Sometimes he would sit until midnight and, leaving my room for the corridor, would say to my mother 'Do not worry, Emilia Aronovna, we and Zhenya are not only talking about history, it is simply very pleasant for me to converse with your son!' He was really very fond of me, and even after he had left our school ('I am sick of teaching musicians!') for over a year he continued to come to us, teaching me, and on principle did not take a kopek for this, however much my parents tried to persuade him. And he would talk to me not only about what was designated in the school programme (to which, incidentally, he far from always adhered), and was very concerned about my general development and world outlook, in order, as he would say, that 'I should not live in the world like a cat in a library that sees the books but has no idea about what is written in them.' Of course he talked with me a lot about what was going on in the country, the stormy events of perestroika, giving me various articles to read and analyse. Viktor Yuryevich himself was interested in absolutely everything and, teaching in our school, regularly attended school concerts, listened to music and, in so far as he could, made sense of everything, asking knowledgeable people (including me) about what was interesting or things he could not understand. After my debut with the Chopin concertos, he said to me that he had the feeling of rose petals falling from on high. From one of the girls in my class I know that to this day he loves music and goes to concerts.

Now, many years later, it is hard to say with certainty, but I think that Viktor Yuryevich played a part in the fact that throughout my conscious life I have always been interested in history and politics. Once, during one of my last meetings with Vladimir Konstantinovich Bukovsky, with whom I often correspond, debating various political questions and arguing, even he, who has devoted his whole life to politics, asked me, 'But why do you interest yourself in precisely this? Why not, for instance, in astronomy?', and I replied that I was not interested in what was going on in the cosmos but on earth, in our life, with us.

Grigory Borisovich Minkin – Teacher of Literature

At the time of our very first lesson Grigory Borisovich told me that he had once written poetry that was even published, and he read me his poem about autumn, which began, as I recall, with the words, 'The beds of nasturtiums are burning like a flare'; in the middle was 'this jasmine that in spring is so fragrant, asks for mercy from the wind'; the last line of each stanza consisted of a single word, 'autumn', and at the very end of the poem were three words: 'autumn quietly rustles'.

And at the time of the final exam on literature, I remember receiving a ticket with a question, about what I do not recall, but I know that I knew the answer. I came forward and prepared to reply, but Grigory Borisovich suddenly said, 'Well, I think Zhenya will have a creative reply,' and suggested I speak about what I wanted to. I talked about my favourite Voloshin and received a top mark.

When, in an essay on Mayakovsky, whom as an adolescent I admired greatly, I wrote, 'the Communist Mayakovsky', Mushroom said to me that Mayakovsky was not a Communist.

'How wasn't he?!'

'He wasn't a member of the Party.'

Well, I, naturally, had not his Party card in mind, but his convictions . . . And in response to my words from the same essay, 'Mayakovsky loved Pushkin, not the dear, charming Pushkin, but Pushkin the revolutionary,' he explained to me that it was wrong to call Pushkin a 'revolutionary', that sometimes Pushkin wrote freedom-loving poems and sometimes loyal poems, that his attitude to the Tsar changed according to the Tsar's attitude to him. This was, of course, completely different from the programme, and I remember that I said nothing in response and did not ask, but with childish naivety was simply shocked: did that mean that Pushkin was without principles?

Only once in my lessons with Grigory Borisovich did we come to a standstill: when he asked me to write an essay on Anatoly Merzlov according to the sketch by Konstantin Simonov.* I simply did not know what to write: well, yes, he was a hero who died heroically, but what could I add to what Simonov had written? I thought and thought and came to a conclusion. In my essay I expanded on the idea that many cowardly people justify their cowardice by mentioning their family and children. Merzlov also had a wife and daughter but was not a coward; he performed a feat and perished. And about cowardly men who justified their unwillingness to face danger demanded by duty by referring to their wife and children, I wrote in a fit of temper: 'And would it be easier for a wife to have such a husband? And for the children would such a father be a good example?' Mushroom read my essay aloud, as he always did, and, coming to that place, commented,

---

* Anatoly Merzlov was a tractor driver who, during the harvest, tried to save the tractor he was working on when a fire broke out in a wheat field. He received fatal burns and died thirteen days later.

'"And would it be easier for a wife to have such a husband" – Well, as a matter of fact . . .' And at this point, it seems that I understood something.

Recently I also found some information about Grigory Borisovich on the Internet: as a teacher of literature for half a century he was proposing that in schools they continue to study Solzhenitsyn and Shalamov. Yes, he is no longer a young man, our Grigory Borisovich . . . G-d give him health and strength.

Comrade Colonel, or Oginski's Polonaise in a Gas Mask

Well, and of course there was our legendary military instructor Georgy Timofeyevich Tushev, 'Comrade Colonel', the terror of all the school, including the director, Zinovy Isaakovich. Everybody was afraid of the military instructor, and throughout the school his aphorisms were passed from mouth to mouth: 'A concert is a private matter, but preliminary military training is a matter of state,' 'Just imagine you are going through wasteland and suddenly from round a corner comes a tank,' and suchlike. Even before I began to study with him, having heard many of his sayings related by older pupils, I used to write epigrams about Comrade Colonel and put them in the shoe bags of my schoolmates which hung in the cloakroom: to my childish imagination it seemed that in this way I was engaging in an underground struggle. These epigrams were, of course, naive and silly, but one day, passing the open door of one of the classrooms, I heard Mishka Lidsky say to someone: 'This is an epigram about the colonel,' quoting a line from it.

Georgy Timofeyevich, incidentally, gradually came to like me, but for this some preparatory work was necessary. He made everyone, including girls, take apart and reassemble a Kalashnikov in a certain number of seconds; some people seriously hurt their fingers, but this did not trouble the colonel at all, and everyone was afraid of saying a word to him: after all, Preliminary Military Training, PMT, was a matter of state! And so when my time came to study PMT and civil defence, Anna Pavlovna set off to talk with Georgy Timofeyevich. She started to tell him how talented I was and so on, and Comrade Colonel looked at her with fish eyes without any reaction. And then Anna Pavlovna said, 'Bear in mind that his hands are national property. He has just been performing in Japan and brought from there five and a half million yen.' Well, for the colonel it was all the same, yen, roubles or pounds, but the number itself naturally made an immense impression on him, and with a completely different facial expression asked: 'How many?'

'Five and a half million,' confirmed Anna Pavlovna, 'Therefore if he hurts his hands, you will bear responsibility for it.'

Comrade Colonel reflected for a few moments and then sadly confirmed: 'Yes . . . he will not do service.'

After that I set off to see him for our first meeting. Initially he was confused and greeted me with the words, 'Hello, Serezha,' and then announced, 'Well, in general, Zhenya, I want you to be not only such a . . . musician, but you ought to be an all-round person. In particular you should have a thorough knowledge of military matters.' He did not make me take apart and reassemble the gun, but demanded that I apply myself to theory and learn how to march. At the end of September, during our first year of studying military matters, he drew our class up in the hall for physical training and began to lead us along in goose step, but just before then I had been touring and had missed several lessons. He said, 'Well, Kissin has been travelling . . . it is difficult for him,' and later, towards the end of the lesson, in front of the whole class he announced the following to me: 'Well, never mind, Zhenya: you study and learn how to march in goose step. It is necessary for you! Because, apart from your sort of playing . . . you have no co-ordination: your right arm and your right leg. But never mind: you will learn and then you will go out onto the platform like tha-at! And then you play like tha-at! So that all women swoon!' I began to study this skill stubbornly, and my father, remembering his army service, trained me . . . and next, a few months later, we went with our school to Tbilisi and I marched onto the stage to play Rachmaninov's Second Piano Concerto with the Tbilisi Philharmonic Orchestra! It was probably due to nerves. Our director of studies, Elena Evgenevna Lysenko, sitting next to Anna Pavlovna, asks her:

'What on earth is he doing?!'

'The colonel trained him!' whispers Anna Pavlovna in reply.

'Well, you must tell him!'

'Yes, I'll tell him of course!'

And when I come into the school after that visit, I meet Elena Evgenevna and she says to me:

'I told the colonel that you came out onto the platform in goose step!' 'And how did he react?' I ask.

'"Well, it was I who trained him!"'

Comrade Colonel also taught us how to put on and take off gas masks. He considered that it would be useful for all pianists to sit through one of our piano lessons in gas masks. One day we put on gas masks in our basement, and on a nearby piano I played a chord. 'Oh!' reacted Georgy Timofeyevich, 'Zhenya, play Oginski's Polonaise.' Well, since the colonel had ordered it, I had to play. 'Boys, has anybody got a camera? No? A pity . . . Otherwise we would have had a fine photograph: Zhenya Kissin playing Oginski's Polonaise in a gas mask.'

In general he liked me in his own way, and I remember at the end of our last meeting he wished me well in playing 'the music of our Fatherland'.

Anna Pavlovna Kantor

Now at last I shall write about my principal teacher, Anna Pavlovna. We were introduced by Evgeny Yakovlevich Lieberman, a well-known pianist and teacher at the Gnessin Institute, a pupil of Heinrich Neuhaus and author of some fine books about pianism. His wife worked in the same music school as my mother, and our families became friendly; he knew me from my early youth, and I later married his daughter. My mother took me to him when I was five, and Evgeny Yakovlevich tried to give me a few lessons, but considered that it would be better for me if at first I were in the hands of a wise and talented children's teacher, and decided to show me to Anna Pavlovna. As my mother did not want me to study music professionally, seeing from the example of Allochka how difficult it was and what physical efforts were needed (and in my childhood I had far from brilliant health), he told Anna Pavlovna about me, agreed on a meeting and only then told my mother about it, saying that she would let him down if she did not ring Anna Pavlovna. Thus my mother had no choice but to ring and take me for an audition at the Gnessin School.

To this day I remember how I first saw my future teacher: we were waiting in the vestibule, and Anna Pavlovna appeared from the right; she was dressed all in green and her left leg was bandaged, having been broken. Anna Pavlovna would often relate afterwards how I then raised my large blue eyes with their long eyelashes to her, and she immediately fell in love with me for all her life. After a certain time I also fell in love with Anna Pavlovna and in my childhood I wanted to marry her. We went into classroom No. 7 and I began to play for her . . . but I do not remember this and am therefore narrating from her stories. I played by ear Chopin's Third Ballade, Liszt's Twelfth Hungarian Rhapsody (the opening octaves with two hands), and excerpts from *The Nutcracker* . . . Then my mother said to Anna Pavlovna that I liked to improvise on themes I was given, and Anna Pavlovna suggested to me, 'Well play about a dark forest . . . and then the sun comes up and the birds sing,' and I played all that. Incidentally, according to the recollections of Anna Pavlovna, in my improvisations I wandered over all possible keys, but in the end always returned to the key in which I had begun. At one moment she said to me,

'Oh what a good piece! Play it again!'

'But I don't remember it,' was my reply.

Anna Pavlovna did not believe me and said:

'Well, play another piece about a forest,' thinking that I would play the same thing, but I really improvised something completely different.

Hearing me, Anna Pavlovna said to my mother:

'I am afraid of teaching this child; he can play by ear Chopin's ballade and Liszt's rhapsody, and I must explain to him how to read music, give him simple little pieces to play – he will be bored.'

Mother replied:

'Don't worry, he won't be bored; he is a very curious boy, he will be interested to find out something new.'

Then Anna Pavlovna invited into the room the director of studies, Elena Evgenevna Lysenko, and the teacher of solfeggio, Ekaterina Georgievna Kruglikova, and I played to them as well, and they immediately admitted me to the school.

In a sense Anna Pavlovna's anxieties were justified. During the first months of study I really did not respond to the simple little pieces that she gave me, and therefore I played them completely indifferently. But when the time came for me to play in the very first test, Anna Pavlovna called my mother to the lesson and said she did not know what to do. At home Mother explained to me that in those children's pieces which I was playing the composers were also telling of something and began to think about exactly what it was, trying to arouse my fantasy. When I played these pieces to Anna Pavlovna at my next lesson, she asked Mother, 'What have you done with him? He is really playing quite differently.' From that time on there were no more 'performing problems' in our lessons. Having learned musical notation, I immediately began to write down my own music. During many lengthy illnesses in childhood I would lie in bed and write piano pieces which I dedicated to 'my

dear, beloved teacher Anna Pavlovna Kantor'. As soon
as I discovered something new, I immediately used it in
my own compositions. Once in my first year I wrote
a little piece called 'Chromatic Étude'; at that time I
already knew 'poco a poco' but did not yet know the
term 'accelerando' and wrote at one place in my piece,
'poco a poco speeding up'! When I returned to Anna
Pavlovna's class after one of my regular illnesses, I was
so restrained on account of my childish shyness that
she said, 'Well, are we going to meet again?' According
to her reminiscences, in the first months of our lessons,
when she explained something to me, I did not react at
all, and then she would begin to explain the same thing
over and over, and I still did not react, and finally she
asked: 'Well, did you understand?'

To which I calmly replied: 'I understood it long ago.'

But after a time I finally 'thawed' and began to ask
Anna Pavlovna: 'When are you coming to our house?'

And thus I took her as my own, as a member of the
family, for the rest of my life.

I think there must be few people in the world of such
integrity as Anna Pavlovna: she devoted her entire life to
teaching, she never had her own family, but with full justification called herself 'a mother with many children'.
It is another question whether all her pupils turned out
later to be 'grateful children', but that is a matter for
their consciences. Anna Pavlovna not only taught me
everything I can do on the piano, but always concerned

herself with my human development. During the years of my study at the Gnessin School all our family grew very close to her, and when she was completely alone we invited her into our family and from that time we lived together.

Her Method

The main aim of Anna Pavlovna's work was always to discover, preserve and develop the individuality of each particular pupil, and for that reason all her pupils, unlike those of some other teachers, always played differently. For example, my very good friend Rustem Hayroudinoff, having studied at the Moscow Conservatoire with the respected professor Lev Nikolayevich Naumov, used to tell me how the latter would strive for Rustem to reflect the character of the music with his face: 'Well, Rustem, well, it should be written on your mug! Otherwise they will say that you are not a real Naumov man!' By contrast Anna Pavlovna never tried to make her pupils look like Kantor people; she wanted us to look like Demidenko, Berlinskaya, Batagov, Kissin, Smirnova, Apekisheva and so on. One of the methods by which she achieved this was that she *never* played during lessons. Deliberately, so that we should not copy her. She always had recourse to words alone to arouse our own fantasy.

As an adolescent I began to play with a harsh sound,

because it seemed to me that it was 'manly'. Moreover, when playing and when I was being photographed I would stick my chin out for the same reason, thinking that I looked more steadfast. Anna Pavlovna put up with all this persistently, continuing to teach me in the same way as before, patiently making observations, and gradually everything sorted itself out. She did not use any special methods even then: just conversations, remarks and patience. However, a few years later, when a week before the death of Claudio Arrau I played for him, he praised Anna Pavlovna, who was present, for teaching me to play *forte* in the same way that his teacher Martin Krause, a pupil of Liszt, had done: using the weight of all of the arm from the shoulder, so that it would sound noble and beautiful.

When I played for the first time with Vladimir Ashkenazy Beethoven's 'Emperor' Concerto, after the first rehearsal he went up to Anna Pavlovna and, having said many good words about my playing, suggested that I play the very beginning of the concerto, the cadenza-like opening, more freely, as if improvising. Anna Pavlovna replied that she absolutely agreed with him and suggested the same thing to me, but it did not sound natural when I did it, and therefore she did not insist on it. Vladimir Davidovich said in a pleasantly surprised tone, 'What a good teacher!'

That attitude was entirely typical of Anna Pavlovna.

And one more important individual feature of her

personality: to this day, having already passed ninety, she continues to learn. A few years ago I decided to learn Barber's sonata, which earlier Anna Pavlovna had been through with Anton Batagov, but nonetheless considered that she did not fully understand this music. Anton was very fond of twentieth-century music, but Anna Pavlovna was not. And so, when I had gone away on a long tour of South-East Asia, she asked musicians whom she knew to obtain for her the music and all the recordings of this sonata that they could find; and she listened to them day after day, in various interpretations with the score in her hands, until she was fully conversant with them. And Anna Pavlovna always encouraged me to study – not only with her, but also from other interpreters, and she herself was always an example of this. When we started to live under one roof, every time I began working on a new programme or a new piece, Anna Pavlovna would always buy all the recordings of the music that she could find; she would begin to study them and then encourage me to do the same thing together with her. During our listening sessions she would always draw my attention to what she thought important and useful. I myself also listened to recordings of pieces I was working on, but not immediately, only after I had learned the pieces myself and had formed my own conception of them. Sometimes Anna Pavlovna would say to me of one recording or another, 'It is not interesting, but nonetheless listen to it: it is useful!'

Elena Somoilovna Ephrussi

And there was yet another teacher in my life, with whom I did not officially study, but who played a large role in my learning of music and who was altogether very dear to me: a teacher at our school called Elena Somoilovna Ephrussi, whom Anna Pavlovna described as her second mother. Elena Somoilovna was once a close friend of the mother of Anna Pavlovna, a piano teacher, Faina Grigoryevna Kantor, who also taught in our school. When in 1960 Faina Grigoryevna died, Anna Pavlovna and Elena Somoilovna, who had never had her own family, began to live together for the next thirty years, right up to the death of Elena Somoilovna. Even when I was very young Elena Somoilovna and I loved each other very much, and she would often say to me, 'You are my little friend.' There were times in my childhood when I was lazy and Anna Pavlovna became very upset and began to wonder whether anything would come of me. Then wise Elena Somoilovna would say to her, 'Believe in him more!' And when Anna Pavlovna could in no way teach me to work on technically difficult passages at a slow speed, the experienced Elena Somoilovna would say, 'That means he is thinking more quickly.'

Sometimes Anna Pavlovna gave me lessons at home, and Mother and I usually remained afterwards 'to drink tea with a cake' which my mother had baked. At that time, Elena Somoilovna, being old and unhealthy, lay in bed for long periods, and I would sit alongside her and entrust her with all my secrets. Her favourite composer was Bach; one day, I remember, I played her the B flat Minor Prelude from the first book of the *Well-Tempered Clavier* and she said, 'If you don't believe in G-d – that will make you believe.'

We often went on holiday together: at first to Estonia in the little town of Haapsalu where, incidentally, Tchaikovsky had also holidayed and subsequently written a cycle of piano pieces, 'Souvenir de Hapsal'; later we went to the Composers' Creativity Homes 'Ruza' and 'Ivanovo'.

Even in the last days of her life Elena Somoilovna, despite her very poor state, worried about me. When she was in hospital dying of cancer, I was lying at home in bed with measles. And Elena Somoilovna's last words were: 'How is Zhenya? How are the measles?'

She was a remarkable teacher and wonderful person, exceptionally kind, pure, decent and full of integrity. She worshipped her profession, she worshipped children, and children unfailingly repaid her in kind. Blessed be her memory!

It is not possible to write about all my teachers, and I hope that those of them whom I have not mentioned will not be offended: I remember you all, am grateful to you all, and love you.

Part II

YOUTH

I do not know how to reply when asked about the main impressions of my youth. It is perhaps even more difficult than replying to the question: Who is your favourite composer/pianist/writer/poet? How is it possible to choose someone or something, when there is so much that is fine in the world? Probably the most important event of youth is youth itself: the unique, wonderful springtime of human life.

Leaving Russia

At the very end of perestroika, in 1991, just at the time of the collapse of the Soviet Union, I was on tour in North America. I gave solo recitals in Toronto, Dallas, Los Angeles, San Francisco, Montreal, Boston and New York. We set off with my mother and Anna Pavlovna, and after my tour was over, my American impresario Charles Hamlen arranged for us work visas for a year and a half, and a few months later my father and Allochka came on tourist visas, but longer visas were obtained for them so that they could stay with us.

In Moscow, incidentally, people had already 'arranged my departure' long before that. Already in 1989 rumours circulated that I was either emigrating or had already departed for the West. I remember how, when I was going for lessons to the Gnessin Institute, a girl I did not know met me in the street and said, 'Hello, Zhenya. Are you leaving us forever?' I was very surprised and said that I was not going anywhere. 'No? Hurrah!' was her reply. And once, after one of my performances, a girl came up and asked me for an interview for, I think, a wall newspaper, and asked, amongst other things, whether it was true that I was going to live abroad. And when in autumn 1989 Vladimir Ashkenazy came to Moscow to give concerts, in the interval of his first concert in the Great Hall of the Conservatoire I met the above-mentioned Lyudmila Nikolayevna Lukovniko-va, and she informed me in her unforgettable smoky bass voice, 'I have just been asked whether Kissin has remained in the FRG? I say, "It's true, especially as he is sitting here at the concert!"'

An Exception to the Rules!

Settling in New York, I enjoyed everything new that life brought me at the time, and look back at that period with great pleasure. For my parents and Anna Pavlovna, of course, it was difficult: they were well past fifty and Anna Pavlovna was nearly seventy; at such an age, to migrate to another country, not knowing the language, is not easy. Naturally, it greatly got on my nerves, taking up a huge amount of time which I should have liked to spend on something considerably more pleasant and interesting, to have to constantly walk around the embassies of various countries, filling in questionnaires and being photographed in order to receive visas, without which I could not tour with a Russian passport. A solution to this problem once and for all could only be achieved by obtaining the citizenship of one of the Western countries, and I had that option. But it was important for me that not only I but my whole family, all five of us, could simultaneously obtain permanent and legal status in the West. This desire of mine went against all standard practices of the time, and for that reason I hoped I would be granted an exception to the rules; and finally my dreams turned into reality. That was a separate, great and very important story in my life which carried on, in its considerable complexity, for ten years.

The House of Lords

In the story of how my family finally managed to obtain indefinite leave to remain, and later British citizenship, the main figure will be a man thanks to whom this happened and who became for me and for all of us one of the dearest people in our lives.

It was in April 1992, a few months after our moving to New York. One fine day my impresario Charles Hamlen came round to talk business, and suddenly started to bow and scrape to us, which looked especially comic on account of his near-two-metre height and thinness. He continued, 'Now I shall talk to you only in that way!' After that, he got a letter out of his briefcase and took from it a yellowish sheet of paper: at the top of it was written in English 'House of Lords', headed by an emblem, and below several paragraphs of text beneath which was the signature 'Lord Kissin'. The author of the letter, addressed to Charles, explained that he had recently heard of a young pianist from Russia, Evgeny Kissin, and he would be interested to know whether they were related. At that time we all simply laughed, but Charles of course replied, and a few weeks later received a second letter from Lord Kissin. In it Lord Kissin wrote that in the 1920s–1930s his uncle had lived in the USSR, working as head of the Organisation for Corn Exports, but was executed at the end of the 1930s. Reading this letter, I, of course, instantly remembered my grandpa's story of Abram Ananyevich Kissin, and it immediately became clear that we had laughed for nothing. Realising that we really were relatives, I myself wrote a letter to Lord Kissin, a few months later rang him, and at the end of August that year we finally met. The meeting took place in the south of France, where he then lived for most of the time and where, a number of kilometres from his estate, I was to give a concert in Menton. Before the start of the concert there was a knock at the door of the green room and a young, dark-haired youth of medium height and with a very pleasant smile entered, held out a visiting card and said in English, 'I am his grandson.' On Lord Kissin's card was written by hand, 'I am here. How and where shall we meet?' I asked the young man to convey to his grandfather an invitation to call on me in the green room after the concert. When the time came, there stood before me the tall, well-built Lord Kissin and with him were his tiny wife, daughter, grandson . . . I no longer remember whether his son-in-law and granddaughter were also there. We exchanged a few pleasantries, and Lord Kissin invited us to lunch the next day. Mother had been particularly struck by the resemblance between Lord Kissin and Uncle Senia, the younger brother of my grandpa, and she told me this when they had all gone. But I did not see the likeness, because Lord Kissin was tall and had a moustache, while Uncle Senia was small and clean-shaven. The next day, during our meeting, everything was finally cleared up: Lord Kissin's father had been born in the same shtetl of Kokhanovo in Belarus where my grandpa had been born and raised, and Lord Kissin and my late grandpa were second cousins!

Over the next five years, right up to his death, we had much contact with Lord Kissin and became friendly with his family, into which he, in the fullest sense of the word, welcomed us; through his connections he also helped us to base ourselves in England. It was difficult: nobody wanted to accept five people, and the British authorities were no exception, but finally Lord Kissin succeeded in persuading them to give the whole family, including Anna Pavlovna, four-year visas with the right, when they expired, to apply for British residence. By the time this happened Lord Kissin was no longer alive, and we were not sure about anything, but nonetheless the right of permanent residence was given us fairly quickly, and in this we were helped by Yehudi Menuhin, himself also a lord. We received British citizenship at the end of 2002.

The History of the Family of Lord Kissin

We became very close to our highly placed relative. He had many interesting things to tell . . . this man's life was colourful and extraordinary. He was born and raised in Danzig, and his family spoke Russian and German. By the time he met us he had already forgotten how to speak Russian, as his mother, the last person with whom he spoke Russian, had died long ago, but he understood practically everything. My mother talked to him in Russian, Lord Kissin replied in English, and they understood each other. In his youth he had studied law at the Universities of Freiburg and Basel. In the Zionist club of Freiburg University he got to know his future wife Ruth; she originated from Berlin, but later all her remaining family in Berlin perished during the Holocaust. For this reason Harry was against the idea of the European Union: 'I did not want to share citizenship with those who killed Ruth's parents!', he told me; many years later, however, he changed his attitude to that project. After their marriage young Ruth and Harry moved to England, and a few years later were joined by his mother, although his father, alas, did not manage to get to England: a refugee in France, he together with other refugees fell off the back of a lorry, received serious head injuries and soon died. Incidentally, he had been friendly with Chagall. Arriving in England, Harry knew no English and gradually learned it from a small dictionary while travelling on the underground. I later asked his daughter Eve whether he had an accent when speaking English, to which she said, 'Not an accent, but intonation.'

Harry, by the way, knew his uncle Abram Ananyevich and, during their last meeting somewhere in Europe in the 1930s, tried to persuade him to remain in the West but, alas, without success. When at the beginning of the 1990s Harry's son Robert went to Moscow as a businessman, he was very touched by being shown the study in which his grandpa twice-removed had worked. Harry had a younger brother, Samuel, who had also come to England and settled there. When, shortly we became acquainted with them, Lord Kissin and his wife came to New York and visited us, we showed them a photograph of my grandpa. Tears came to Harry's eyes, and he said to his wife, 'Look, he really is a copy of my brother!' In his youth Samuel was a Trotskyist, but broke with Trotsky after the founder of the Fourth International, on seeing Samuel's pregnant wife, announced, 'I do not like ugly women.'

In 1939, when the threat of World War II was in the air, Samuel said to his brother, 'What, do you think I am going to take part in an imperialist war?!', but when shortly afterwards he heard of the pact between Hitler and Stalin, on the next day he signed up for the British army! Harry himself served in the British secret service during the war and after. He did not tell me much about that, but I remember how when I once told him that I had been reading a book about Kim Philby, he replied briefly, with a significant half-smile, 'I was in that department! But I didn't know about Philby, no . . .'

Having arrived in England with nothing, Harry gradually prospered there, becoming an important businessman, a banker, a member of the Labour Party, a friend and adviser to Harold Wilson while the latter was prime minister, and, finally, a lord, one of the first Jews to be granted such a title. He was very fond of music and art in general, was a member of the management of Covent Garden and sponsored various cultural projects in Israel. Having become a lord, he left the Labour Party for, as he explained to me, 'Here the party rules are far stricter than in America, and I did not want to be committed to any religion.' I remember how, when the House of Lords had to vote on the Maastricht Treaty,

Lord Kissin flew especially from the south of France to London in order to vote for the first time against his former party: the Labourists made the so-called social chapter a condition for accepting the Treaty, and Lord Kissin was against it: 'They think this a socialist principle. I am basically a socialist, but I do not consider that it is a socialist principle. I am convinced that, if a person wants to work more than eight hours a day, why forbid him to do so? It is very difficult for me to vote for a government that I dislike so much, which has made so many mistakes, but I must do it, because the Maastricht Treaty is a great deal, and we must not let it be sunk.'

The country which Harry Kissin chose as his second native land gave him more than one reason to be proud. In his time, he had some kind of business in Yugoslavia, and when he went there wherever he walked he was constantly followed at a few metres' distance by agents of the local security services: they were keeping an eye on 'an enemy'. And then, late one evening, the telephone in his London flat rang: on the line was one of those with whom Lord Kissin had had dealings in Yugoslavia, an old comrade-in-arms of Tito, who said that he was now in London and wanted to come to see him immediately. They sat together the whole night through, and this man told Lord Kissin that he could no longer stand all the crimes of the Communist regime nor take part in them; he wanted to stay in England. Lord Kissin helped him in this, and sometime later, when he was not at home, the British security services rang and told his wife, who answered the phone, 'Please tell your husband to tell his friend that, if he walks along the embankment, he should not go too near the river, and if he is using the underground, let him not go too near to the platform edge.' Lord Kissin was very proud of this: when he himself used to visit Yugoslavia the local security services followed him like an enemy, but when a Yugoslav escaped to England, the British security services were concerned to preserve his life!

This man did much in his life, travelled to many places. At the beginning of the 1990s he went to Russia to look in the KGB's archive for materials about his uncle. He used to tell us that when he arrived in Moscow and opened his mouth to speak Russian after a break of several decades, he discovered in a few seconds that he was speaking Italian!

Lord Kissin died in November 1997. As early as the time when we got to know him he had cancer (I remember how he told me about it completely calmly), and this was the cause of his death. His wife, a tiny woman with an iron spirit, outlived him by many years, reaching the age of ninety-nine; to the end of her life she visited a swimming pool, smoked several packets of cigarettes a day and bequeathed her body to a hospital in the south of France for scientific research.

Telling friends about Lord Kissin, my mother always said, 'He was not simply handsome – he was brilliant.'

And he really was brilliant: clever, educated, intelligent, with aristocratic manners – although not by blood, he was a real lord! And when he was already over eighty, my London manager, then the forty-year-old Jilly Clarke, once remarked, 'Oh, he has such a sparkle in his eyes!' And he was a very kind, cordial and warm-hearted man. Blessed be his memory.

The Beginning of Life in the West

And so, to return to our departure from Russia, my tours in America and Canada had come to an end in October 1991. I opened an account in one of the New York banks and put the money I had earned into it; Charles had arranged visas – but, after all, we had to live somewhere! In this Charles also helped: one of his friends, a conductor of Broadway shows who at the time was in Los Angeles, was letting his flat, which was situated on Manhattan's Upper West Side, at the corner of 75th Street and Columbus Avenue. Through the mediation of Charles we rented it and moved in. The Steinway firm without delay very kindly let me borrow, without charge, one of their baby grand pianos – and, by the way, continued to do so for many years until recently, when I at last bought a piano from them. The flat was fully furnished, and in it I found quite a number of books and recordings; since we lived there for eleven months, I had time to acquaint myself with many of them. Of the recordings, I was particularly interested in a box of compact discs issued on the occasion of the centenary of the best orchestra in America, the Chicago Symphony, made over the years and featuring various outstanding conductors. To this day I have two cassettes onto which I copied the recordings from this collection that particularly interested me: Brahms's Academic Festival Overture conducted by Hindemith, Hindemith's Symphonic Metamorphosis on Themes of Carl Maria von Weber conducted by Kubelík, Lutosławski's Third Symphony conducted by Solti, Bartók's Suite from *The Miraculous Mandarin* conducted by Kertész, Kodály's *Dances of Galánta* conducted by Reiner, Kodály's *Psalmus Hungaricus* conducted by Solti, Bartók's *Hungarian Sketches* conducted by Reiner, and Franck's *Rédemption* and *Le Chasseur Maudit* conducted by Désiré Defauw. Onto one of these cassettes I also copied a pair of Toscanini's recordings from our host's audio library: the Suite from Kodály's *Háry János*, and Leopold Mozart's 'Toy' Symphony. All these compositions were unfamiliar to me at that time and so it was interesting to get to know them. Of the books that were at my disposal, I read avidly the memoirs of Arthur Rubinstein (especially the first volume) and of Galina Vishnevskaya; the latter I had read in Russian recently while still in Moscow, and so reading them in English translation greatly helped me to learn the language. And two other books from our hosts' library I naturally read from cover to cover: an American bestseller of the 1970s, a two-volume illustrated book with the title *The Joy of Sex*.

Later I began to buy books in New York, and gradually built up my own library. First of all, of course, I was interested in the history of the country in which I had settled: the memoirs of Franklin, de Tocqueville's *Democracy in America* and *The Federalist*, Martin Luther King's *Why We Can't Wait*, and the *Report of the National Advisory Commission on Civil Disorders* (1967); and one admirer gave me Kennan's *Memoirs*. But I was also interested in the history of other countries: to this day there stand in my New York bookcase volumes I had acquired at that time: Villehardouin and Joinville's *Chronicles of the Crusades*, Plumb's *England in the Eighteenth Century* . . . In those days I had little money, and so bought cheap books that were sold in the street. But in the summer of 1992, while in Germany, I remember finding on a street bookstand in Kiel a number of books in Russian: Al. Ginzburg's book on the trial of Sinyavsky and Daniel; the memoirs of Pyotr Yakir, *Childhood in Prison*; W. Leonhard's *Betrayal: The Hitler–Stalin Pact of 1939* and S. Swianiewicz's *In the Shadow of Katyn: Stalin's Terror*. I arrived in New York at the beginning of that year with a book by N. Cohn, *Warrant for Genocide*: it had been given to me by Viktor Yuryevich, who came to my concert in Moscow at the end of 1991.

I worked a great deal, studying Beethoven's 'Emperor'

Concerto and his Choral Fantasy, the Third Piano Concerto and Preludes by Rachmaninov, Schumann's Piano Concerto and Fantasy, Balakirev's *Islamey*, Prokofiev's Fourth Piano Sonata . . . While I was battling with the difficulties of *Islamey*, Debbie, an elderly black woman who was cleaning our flat, suddenly asked me, 'What is that music you are playing?' I showed her the score. 'Very good,' she said approvingly.

My Acquaintance with James Levine

Soon after our move to New York I was contacted by Tom, the brother of James Levine, the distinguished conductor and artistic director of the Metropolitan Opera; Tom looks after all his brother's affairs. Levine had heard of me and wanted to meet and discuss possible collaboration in future. We met, got on very well, and Levine began to invite me to his performances in the Metropolitan Opera; thus I heard live his *L'Elisir d'Amore*, *Traviata*, *Elektra* and many other operas. I well remember how we all first went to *Aida* at the Metropolitan Opera, which was being conducted by some little-known maestro, and on the next day heard *L'Elisir d'Amore* conducted by Levine: it was as if two different orchestras had been playing! Later he sent me as a present a large cardboard box with many of his recordings, in which he performed as both a conductor and as a pianist – he is also a fine performer of chamber music. Amongst them were many works I did not then know, for instance the Quintets for Piano and Wind Instruments by Mozart and Beethoven, Strauss's *Metamorphosen* . . . and I listen to these recordings to this day, enjoying and learning from them. And I shall never forget how at our first meeting Levine, questioning me about my immediate plans, commented on them with great warmth, referring to his colleagues by their first names: 'Are you playing that with Claudio?* Great! And you're playing that with Seiji?† Great!' And in this way he won me over as a person.

I have collaborated with many remarkable conductors, but of those who are at present alive, closest of all to me is Levine. There is a certain amazing similarity not only in the way we both understand, but also naturally feel, music. We have played a variety of the repertoire together: Beethoven's Second, Fourth and Fifth Piano Concertos, both concertos by Chopin, Brahms's two piano concertos, Rachmaninov's Second . . . Several times we have played together Schubert's music for two pianos: the F minor Fantasy, 'Lebensstürme' and the C major Duo; our concert with this programme at Carnegie Hall was recorded on compact disc, and since then Levine has several times told me that it is the favourite of all his recordings and that he often listens to it.

---

* Claudio Abbado (1933–2014), an outstanding Italian conductor.
† Seiji Ozawa (b. 1935), an outstanding Japanese conductor.

This man is not simply a Musician with a capital letter, but a musician to the core: he in a literal and full sense lives in music and by music.

Harold Schonberg, Music Columnist of *The New York Times*

During the first year of my life in America, I met several times with the famous music critic Harold Schonberg, who for several decades was a leading columnist on *The New York Times*. I first met him during my very first visit to America: he, as it turned out, had heard me back in Moscow in 1984, had enjoyed my playing and expressed the wish to interview me. A year later, when he learned that I was staying in New York, he decided to write a long article about me in *The New York Times Magazine*, several times invited me to his home and gave me a copy of his book *The Great Pianists* with a short but very flattering dedicatory inscription, and in one of the last chapters I was also mentioned. In this book I read for the first time an excerpt, several pages long, from the reminiscences of Anton Schindler with a detailed description of how Beethoven, when performing his own sonatas, constantly changed the tempo in correspondence with changes in the moods of the music. In Russia, however, even amongst some very good and respected musicians there is to this day a strong prejudice that 'the Viennese classics should always be played at the same tempo'.

Harold Schonberg also gave me a couple of audio cassettes with various old recordings of outstanding pianists, which he thought might be interesting to me. He was of course an exceptional man, possessing a sharp mind and an even sharper tongue, speaking and writing exactly what he thought without any restraint. 'I have,' he would say to me, 'crazy ideas about Mozart. Mozart was a classical composer, right? So he should be played "classically", right? You see, now everyone is so obsessed with playing Mozart "classically" that they forget that Mozart was a man. Have you read Mozart's letters? You know he writes in particular about rubato* in the performance of his music. Have you heard anybody play Mozart with rubato nowadays? But Mozart wrote about it in his letters. I,' continued Schonberg, 'often have to sit on the jury of various piano competitions. They play a wide variety of music, but as soon as Mozart is heard, all the members of the jury immediately . . .' and here he demonstrated the pose and facial expression of hands crossed on their chests, palms under their arms, lips squeezed together, with the upper lip slightly protruding. 'Everyone thinks they know how to play Mozart. And one day I was sitting with a member of the jury at dinner after one of the sessions, and he says:

---

* **Rubato**, tempo rubato (literally 'stolen time', from the Italian *rubare* 'to steal') – is a musical term indicating temporary freedom, the possibility of increasing or decreasing speed in accordance with the inner requirements of the performer.

"How terribly they played Mozart today, didn't they?"

Then I ask him: "Tell me, who of the currently living pianists plays Mozart in a way you find satisfactory?"'

At this point Schonberg expressively demonstrated how his companion first rested his face on one elbow in deep meditation, then on the other one, then on both, and finally, after lengthy and strained reflection, he exclaimed: '"Edwin Fischer!"

"For goodness sake!" I say, "Edwin Fischer died several decades ago!" But if anyone nowadays played Mozart like Edwin Fischer they would put him in jail!'

Another time he told me, 'People often say: "Yes, he plays Liszt well, but you cannot judge a musician only by how he plays Liszt: you need to hear their performances of Mozart and Beethoven."

But I always reply thus: "Then you cannot judge a pianist by their interpretation of Mozart and Beethoven; you must listen to how they play Liszt."

And everybody thinks I am crazy, but I am right!'

Of course, some of Schonberg's tastes were very specific, and I could not only share, but even understand them. For instance, one of his most favourite pianists was Josef Hofmann. As for my attitude to this great virtuoso . . . I remember when, still a child, I heard a recording of Hofmann playing the first theme of the first movement of Chopin's First Piano Concerto, and I experienced a feeling that I could not express, in so far as I did not know the appropriate word, but I remember very well precisely what it was that I felt, and now I can explain it clearly: I was so touched to the depths of my soul by this music that Hofmann's fast and basically empty performance of this poignant theme seemed to me blasphemous. Such were my intuitive feelings from childhood, and they corresponded to the words of David Rabinovich in his outstanding book *Artist and Style: Problems of Pianist Style*, on which I was brought up: 'Pianistic art, including the *culture of listening*, was destined to be led forward by Rachmaninov and Busoni, but not "the king of pianists" Hofmann.' For me this was always so obvious that I cannot, I admit, to this day understand how such an expert in the history of pianism could place Hofmann so high, especially considering the fact that for several decades in his reviews Schonberg mercilessly criticised Leonard Bernstein, accusing him of superficiality. I can fully understand such a reaction to Bernstein's art, but, compared with Hofmann, Bernstein was simply a philosopher! Incidentally, I had a similar feeling of blasphemy listening to Horowitz's performance of Chopin's Mazurka in B flat minor, about which Schonberg once said to me, 'You probably don't like it? I like it,' and he sang Horowitz's 'little pauses' in this mazurka.

In February 1993 I played a recital of works by Chopin in Carnegie Hall. The recital was recorded by BMG Classics, and the next day I added a few mazurkas, and two discs appeared about six months later with this recording. Soon after the recital Schonberg invited me to lunch at his club. We had a very pleasant conversation together and then rode home in a taxi – and in farewell, as I was leaving the car, Schonberg said to me, 'You just keep playing Chopin this way and don't change!' That was our last meeting.

On Slow Tempi

At the end of 1991 I played Beethoven's Fantasy with Claudio Abbado and the famous Berlin Philharmonic Orchestra as part of their New Year Concert, which was broadcast throughout the Western world as well as being recorded on disc and video. I played well then; in a review there was the following phrase: 'Kissin plays as if his whole life depends on it.' This Fantasy is far from being my favourite piece, but if I were to return to it I should play it rather differently: in faster tempi, and the beginning more like an improvisation. In those years (the end of the 1980s and beginning of the 1990s) I generally liked to play at slow tempi: such was the fashion then and this influenced me. Karajan conducted that way, and Bernstein, and Giulini: the greatest giants . . . so I thought that was how it should be done. On the other hand this was also on account of my desire to play deeply, to say much through the music. As Bruno Walter rightly wrote, in youth performing musicians tend to slower tempi than in old age, because it is easier for the young at such tempi to say everything they want through the music. Incidentally, half a century later this was not the case with the above-mentioned great conductors. Schonberg, by the way, often told me (and not only me, as I later learned) that in recent decades people had begun to play in far slower tempi than before, and that pedagogues were teaching it to their pupils, explaining to them that the slower you play, the deeper the content achieved.

And Beethoven's 'Emperor' Concerto is, of course, a significantly more complex work than the Fantasy, and it took me several years to find myself in this music.

Schumann and Giulini

I did not master Schumann's Piano Concerto at once. When I had begun to study it, one of my American friends asked me on the telephone whether it was difficult for me, and I replied, 'No!'; a few months later I realised what a fool I had been, how deceptive is the apparent easiness of the Schumann concerto. The second theme of the first movement (animato): here under no circumstances can you simply go ahead, that would sound primitive! It must be anxious breathing. And when in the piano part the theme appears with constantly alternating modulations, one must, with the help of these modulations, all the time go 'forward and backward', then this theme will reveal itself in all its richness and beauty.

It was precisely the Schumann Piano Concerto that in spring 1992 my favourite conductor, Carlo Maria Giulini, wanted me to play with the Amsterdam Concertgebouw Orchestra. Still living in Moscow, I had brought back from Japan a device which was both a tape recorder and a radio. After that I began to look at the newspaper in advance for programmes on our music channel and to record from the radio onto my tape recorder everything that interested me. I still have many cassettes with fine recordings from that time, and in particular I recorded a concert in memory of Karajan, in which Giulini performed the second movement of Schubert's 'Unfinished' Symphony and Bruckner's Ninth. It was all completely overwhelming. Generally speaking, the mastery of Giulini is exactly what is dearest of all to me in art: simplicity, depth and spirituality. If one goes beyond the realm of music, that is precisely what I find in Rembrandt; out of the whole, immensely rich collection of New York's Metropolitan Museum my single favourite picture of all is Rembrandt's *Aristotle with the bust of Homer*.

In his manner Giulini was a true aristocrat, a gentleman. I remember how, during our very first meeting in the green room of the magnificent hall of the Amsterdam Concertgebouw, after I had played to Giulini the Schumann Concerto, we were sitting on chairs and couches when he began to talk on various subjects. At that time the great elderly maestro began to complain that in recent years the status of a woman had changed: earlier she had seen herself as a wife and mother, but now young girls are only concerned about making a career for themselves. He regretted that nowadays many girls go about in trousers. 'I do not like it, but OK. But these trousers also have holes in them!' Giulini was distressed that today children spend all their time on computers and do not even know how to draw. And he told me how, one day meeting a major scholar, a Nobel Prize winner, he asked him: 'Where are we going with all this scientific progress?'

The other said: 'I don't know.'

But when Giulini conducted, with the movements of his hands he did not tell the orchestral players how to play, but asked them – and they happily did everything he requested and the result was wonderful.

One of the most exciting episodes of my life was connected with Carlo Maria Giulini. In May 1992 my tour of Germany with the Lithuanian Chamber Orchestra, under the splendid Saulius Sondeckis, was coming to an end, and on the day before our last concert in Frankfurt I was contacted by a representative of Sony Classical who said, 'In a few days' time there are due to be three concerts in Vienna by the Vienna Philharmonic Orchestra under Giulini. The violinist Salvatore Accardo should have been the soloist, but he has fallen ill. Since you have recently played with Giulini the Schumann Concerto, would you like to stand in for Accardo? We are going to record these concerts.' And at that stage I had never played with the Vienna Philharmonic Orchestra. Of course I gladly agreed, but then I still had a Soviet passport, and obtaining visas took a great deal of time – but since it was a matter of performing with the Vienna Philharmonic, the problem was solved at the highest level: the next day before the rehearsal they took my passport, and at the end of the rehearsal returned it with an Austrian visa.

And so the morning after the last concert with the Lithuanians I fly not to New York but to Vienna; they take me straight from the airport to the Musikverein, the orchestra is already on the platform, the rehearsal begins and we play, without stopping, the first movement of the Schumann Concerto – and after the final chords of the first movement the Vienna Philharmonic applauds me! I thought afterwards: those are the moments that make life worth living. Several years later I again came to play the same concerto with Giulini in Rome with the Orchestra of Santa Cecilia. Not long before that his wife had died, and how he had weakened . . . Being a great musician, he could still conduct very well, but it was visible that Giulini was in a deep depression. He had so loved his partner in life, who had been a devoted wife to him, the mother of his children and his manager: she had dedicated her whole life to him.

Herbert von Karajan

There are in life rare moments, hours and days when you think of yourself as being, as they say in Russian, 'in the seventh heaven'. One such day for me was 9 August 1988, when I first met Herbert von Karajan.

At that time I was touring in Switzerland and Austria with the 'Moscow Virtuosi'. These tours were organised by the Munich impresario Hans-Dieter Göhre. Hearing how I played, he sent several of my recordings to Karajan, whom he knew, and wrote to him that I would soon be in Salzburg. Travelling from Zürich to Salzburg, Göhre told me that Karajan had expressed a wish to meet me and that such a meeting could take place the next day after our concert with the 'Virtuosi'. And now, on the morning of 9 August, I was warming up in auditorium 447 of the Salzburg Festspielhaus (to this day I always practise there when I am in Salzburg), and Karajan was due to come at 11.30. I was very nervous of course – everyone gets extremely worked up. Suddenly the door opens and in comes Spivakov.

'Volodya. You here?!' asks Anna Pavlovna in astonishment, 'After all you should already be on the way to Vienna with your orchestra!'

'When such a thing happens, I must be present!' replies Vladimir Teodorovich.

At 11.30 can be heard the sound of the lift doors

opening and the noise of the feet of a large group
of people. A few seconds later the door of the room
opens and in comes or, more accurately, is brought,
for by then he could no longer walk, Karajan. I do not
even remember who the people were who came with
him, I only remember his wife and the photographer
from Deutsche Grammophon. Karajan was dressed in
a casual dark-blue suit and wearing dark glasses. We
greeted each other. Although Karajan could not walk
any more, his handshake was firm. We all sat down, and
I went over to the piano, which was a few metres from
the chairs arranged in three rows. Auditorium 447 is
spacious, and is used for ballet rehearsals; incidentally,
the Bösendorfer on which I played to Karajan stands
there to this day. I began to play Chopin's Fantasy . . .
later Anna Pavlovna said that I had never played it so
well (although I had played it for more than four years
already). I finished playing. Silence. I stand up, take a
few steps towards the audience and suddenly Karajan
blew me a kiss. I draw closer to him, and see that there
are no longer dark glasses on his face and he is wiping
away tears with a handkerchief. I shall never be able
to describe in words my state at that instant. Let my
readers try to imagine for themselves what was going
on in my heart.

Well, and so later Karajan said to me, in English:
'More!'

'May I play Liszt's Twelfth Hungarian Rhapsody?'

I had hardly finished speaking when Karajan replied: 'Whatever you want!'

I played the Rhapsody, rose and saw that the dark glasses were again on Karajan's face; he got up from his chair and tried to walk. I moved nearer to him, several people who had come with him began to help, but Karajan said he wanted to talk to me privately by the piano. Then Spivakov, who was sitting nearby, said that he knew German and would help with translation, and the three of us sat by the piano. Karajan asked whether I played Brahms's Second Piano Concerto, and, receiving a reply in the negative, wanted to know whether I was prepared to learn it, to which, naturally, I said 'Yes.' I do not remember in detail what happened next. It seems that gradually all those present were approaching us. I also played Bach's Siciliana in the arrangement by Kempff, and the beginning of the last movement of Rachmaninov's Second Piano Concerto, after which Karajan asked me to play the end of it and then said: 'You must play it with me here in Salzburg in the summer,' thinking, of course, of the summer of the following year. His wife Eliette said to us: 'I have been living with my husband for thirty years, and have never seen him so touched!' Our meeting lasted exactly an hour. At 12.30 everybody rose to leave. Karajan shook my hand and that of Anna Pavlovna in farewell, but, squeezing the hand of my mother, said, pointing at me: 'Genius.' What a day that was – one of the most memorable and cherished days in my life.

A month and a half later I received an invitation to play Tchaikovsky's First Piano Concerto with Karajan and the Berlin Philharmonic Orchestra in their New Year concert. Arriving in Berlin a few days before the end of the year, I came to the hall of the Berlin Philharmonic, and an hour before the beginning of the first rehearsal with the orchestra we met with Karajan on the platform for me to play to him, and immediately the great maestro made an 'introductory speech': 'I have read documents according to which it was said that after the first performance of his concerto Tchaikovsky said it was too fast. And now everybody plays this concerto very quickly and there is no music. But we are going to make music. You played in Salzburg like nobody else, the acoustics here are excellent – we shall make music!' I began to play, and throughout the entire concerto Karajan constantly interrupted, saying: 'Slower!' Naturally, at that time I did not dare to object, and at our first rehearsal with the orchestra Tchaikovsky's thirty-five-minute concerto lasted fifty minutes! I was in shock; after the rehearsal the orchestral players expressed their dissatisfaction loudly, and the organiser of those concerts on 30 and 31 December, Dorothea Schlösser, said to me: 'Don't worry, he is a crazy old man!' but, of course, nobody could do anything. I think that Karajan's age also made itself felt: after all, at the age of eighty a person's heart beats more slowly, and in his striving not to play too quickly he had simply gone to a different extreme.

What was to be done? The sound engineer Michel Glotz, also a well-known impresario, who was recording those concerts for audio and video, with a broadcast of our New Year concert being screened throughout Europe and a day later in America, said: 'We can persuade Karajan to slightly increase his tempi, but only if Kissin does not rush. Because if he does rush, Karajan will immediately begin to hold back the tempi.' But I felt a natural need to play in a more lively manner precisely because it was awkward playing at such slow tempi, so the result was a vicious circle. But in the end someone told Karajan that I felt uncomfortable playing that way, and I even managed to persuade him to listen to me again. Karajan was very sweet and kept saying, 'I am not your enemy; I am your friend,' and in the end it was possible to find some sort of compromise: the final version of Tchaikovsky's First Piano Concerto issued by Deutsche Grammophon lasted forty minutes.

And all the same, regardless of the inconvenience caused by consistently slow tempi, there emanated from Karajan such magnetism that later Anna Pavlovna told me that in Tchaikovsky's concerto I did things which I had never done before: such was the force of personality on me of this genius. And it was clear to me that if anybody else had conducted at such a slow speed it would have sounded like a caricature, but Karajan filled these tempi with all the forces of his genius. And Yury Temirkanov, having heard the recording Karajan and I made, said it was just as if the dust had been removed from a fine old painting, and it had again appeared before people in all its beauty. When, several years later, I played with Kurt Sanderling, he said to me: 'The only time I was satisfied with a performance of Tchaikovsky's First Piano Concerto was when you played it with Karajan!' Therefore when some people, infinitely less significant than Karajan, Sanderling and Temirkanov, begin to turn up their noses at Karajan's slow tempi, I, to be honest, simply feel pity for them, and recall a scene from Bach's cantata 'Der Streit zwischen Phoebus und Pan', in which Midas, having just demonstrated his undeveloped musical taste, announces in his defence, 'But that's the way I hear it!', to which they reply, 'Yes you have cloth ears!' Faina Grigoryevna Ranevskaya, the great Russian actress, was completely right that the *Mona Lisa* can choose for herself on whom she makes an impression and on whom she doesn't. And, quite rightly, Karajan said to me at that time that 'When they play quickly and there is no music of any kind – it is shit.' Simple, rude – and absolutely right!

A couple of months later, in March 1989, Karajan and I, with the Berlin Philharmonic, again played Tchaikovsky's First Piano Concerto twice: this time at the Salzburg Easter Festival. And in July the whole musical world was shaken by the sad news of this great

conductor's death. I was immediately invited to Salzburg to take part in a memorial concert for Karajan;
in August I went there and visited his grave. Since that
time this charming small town where Mozart was born
has been associated for me with Karajan: on my first
visit I made the acquaintance of Karajan and played
for him, on the second I played with the great maestro
himself, and on the third performed at a concert in his
memory. To this day Eliette Karajan comes to my concerts in Salzburg and reminisces about our first meeting
on that August morning in 1988.

Evgeny Svetlanov

The art of the great musician Evgeny Fyodorovich
Svetlanov, the chief features of which are emotionality and a creative nature, is very close to my heart.
Unfortunately we did not manage to communicate as
much as I should have liked, but each of our meetings,
each time we played together is for me cherished and
unforgettable.

I first saw Evgeny Fyodorovich Svetlanov in the flesh
when I was still a teenager in the middle of the 1980s,
in the Great Hall of the Moscow Conservatoire. If
memory does not deceive me, I was going down the
performers' staircase while he was coming up it, deep
in thought. It was clear to me, as to any musician, that
he was buried in thought not about himself but about

the music that he was about to create. Anybody, even if they were far from music and did not know who was coming up the stairs, seeing Evgeny Fyodorovich at that moment would immediately realise that this was an exceptional man, not a 'simple mortal'.

In November 1986 I took part in a gala concert for the State Orchestra in the Great Hall of the Conservatoire. At that time I played a mazurka and an étude by Scriabin, with success. Unfortunately, I was not able even to see Evgeny Fyodorovich, who was sitting on the platform far from the piano, but I shall never forget the words said to me after my short performance by one of the organisers of the gala: 'Svetlanov was sitting as if under a spell!' I could not have dreamed of such a thing: at that time Evgeny Svetlanov was for me simply something unattainable.

And a few years later, in 1990, our collaboration began. The most memorable of our first performances together was at a concert with the State Orchestra in Toulouse, when we played Tchaikovsky's First Piano Concerto. That was one of those evenings when, as musicians say, you hit the bull's eye: everything worked, and there was some exceptional fusion both with the music and with each other. Evgeny Fyodorovich was very pleased and said that I reminded him of himself in his youth! After the interval Tchaikovsky's Third Symphony was performed. I recall that from childhood I had the stereotype in my head that the Third

Symphony was, so to speak, 'the least successful' of all the symphonies of Pyotr Ilyich, and up to that evening in Toulouse my attitude to it corresponded to that stereotype. But Svetlanov conducted so colourfully and with such inspiration that I simply fell in love with that music – and love it to this day. As encores there were the Adagio from *The Nutcracker* and 'The Dance of the Tumblers' from *The Snow Maiden*: a real firework! From that concert came the feeling of pure joy.

A creative nature . . . Without comparing myself to anyone, from childhood I know from my own experience what it is, and it has always been especially dear and close to me in the art of performance, and not only in that. Such musicians as a rule (although, as is well known, there are no rules without exceptions, which in turn confirm these rules) play/sing/conduct better before a live audience than in recording studios; they cannot perform the same work exactly the same way twice, and if they have to play the same music twice in succession, it simply cannot be on an equally high level. Artur Schnabel was like that: during a recording of Beethoven's Fourth Piano Concerto when, after a very musically successful version, despite a few technical blemishes, either the conductor or the sound engineer suggested that he play it once more, arguing that it would be better, Schnabel replied, 'Perhaps it may be better – but it will never be that good!' Vladimir Sofronitsky was the same, as is witnessed not only by the reminiscences of those who had the chance to listen to him in live concerts, but also by his many recordings – especially if one compares recordings of concert performances with those made in the studio, which he himself called 'my corpses'.

Arturo Benedetti Michelangeli, on the other hand, was the exact opposite: he was a perfectionist. Heinrich Gustavovich Neuhaus, a professor at the Moscow Conservatoire and teacher of Svyatoslav Richter, aptly remarked about his playing, 'Perfection is not only a positive thing, but can also be negative.' And once, after a recital in London (the recital was recorded, but Michelangeli did not permit the recording to be issued, and it came into the world only after his death), he, contrary to his usual manner, played very freely and creatively – as the English say, 'he let himself go'. Michelangeli himself announced, 'Today I played like a prostitute – but a very expensive one!' However, it was precisely because of his perfectionism that he often cancelled recitals at the very last moment, feeling that on that day he would not be able to play in the way he wanted.

Evgeny Fyodorovich Svetlanov was a creative person to the depths of his being. I remember how, a few months after the concert in Toulouse mentioned above, a broadcast was made of his performance of Tchaikovsky's Third Symphony with the State Symphony Orchestra – it was as if quite different music was

My grandparents

With Father

With Mother

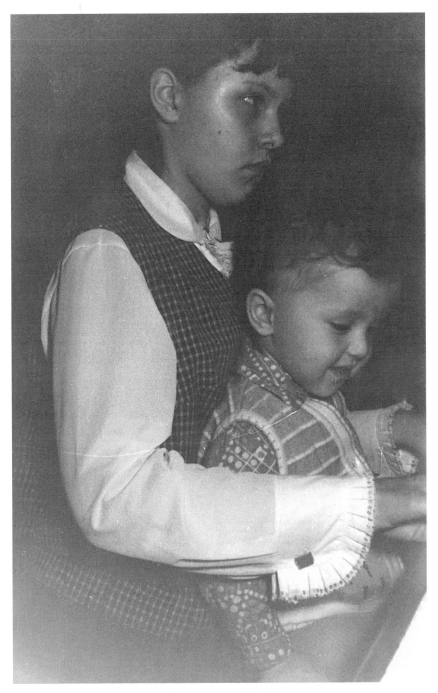

With my sister Allochka

Хоромы
для
ПРИНЦА
Тише!!!
Тише!!! Тише!!!

Father's picture welcoming the newborn son to the house

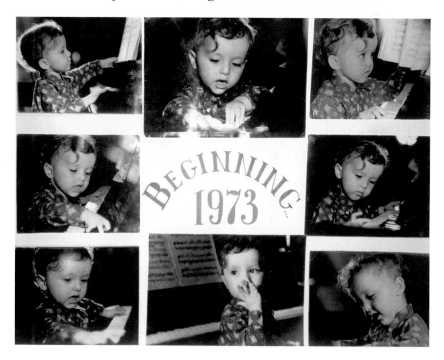

1973

First try

At the piano, three years old

Summer holidays outside Moscow

With Dmitry Kitayenko and Anna Kantor at the rehearsal of
my debut with the two Chopin Concerti in Moscow

In Zvenigorod on the day after my debut

With Anna Pavlovna Kantor in Moscow, May 1984

Right Elena Somoilovna Ephrussi

With Galina Ulanova and Irina Antonova in Moscow, December 1985

Фестиваль „Русская зима"
и
Жене Виртуозам Москвы

Большой зал консерватории

Ни пуха!
ни пера!

Шопен
Шуберт

КОНЦЕРТ

28/XII-1985

Father's picture

Above With Herbert von Karajan in Berlin, December 1988

With the widow of Herbert von Karajan, Eliette, in Salzburg

The family soon after the transition to the USA

With Mother and Lord and Lady Kissin at their house in Valbonne, France

With Prince Charles

Left and below With James Levine in Verbier

With Princess Margaret

With Queen Elizabeth

With Tikhon Khrennikov in Moscow

Above With Seiji Ozawa
in Tanglewood

With Martha Argerich
and Vadim Repin

With Frédéric Mitterrand

With Isaac Stern and Marthe Keller

With Van Cliburn

With the Prince of Holland and his wife

Above With Zubin Metha in Jerusalem,
December 2006

Yakov Rubinstein, who taught history in my school

With Evgeny Svetlanov in Colmar, July 1995

With Yuri Temirkanov in St Petersburg

With Admiral Michael Mullen, Tony Blair, and Rupert Murdoch

being played! I became rather sad . . . and I understood that with such a person as Svetlanov it could not be otherwise: in order to create a masterpiece, apart from difficult and painstaking work, it was necessary to have the public, an essential feeling of actual creation! In June 1996 Evgeny Fyodorovich and I played Rachmaninov's Third Piano Concerto two days running, in Birmingham and in London. The Birmingham concert was as successful as the Toulouse one had been a few years before, 'hitting the bull's eye'. Evgeny Fyodorovich, knowing both himself and me, said, 'It will be worse tomorrow!' And it really was worse, because it could not be the same again. Externally everything was fine, but something important was missing which cannot be created specially, however much you try.

I was lucky enough to be at Svetlanov's concerts when he was at the height of his powers. I shall never forget his performance of Scriabin's *Poème d'extase*: it really was a 'poem of ecstasy' in the full sense of the words, and all the audience (the great majority of whom could not have known this difficult music, for the concert was in France at the Colmar Festival) rose to their feet after the last chord. Also unforgettable was how at that same festival Svetlanov conducted Mahler's First Symphony; how original and amazing in its inner power his interpretation was. I also remember in Colmar Svetlanov's performance of Brahms's First Symphony. Before that, in 1992, I had occasion to hear three days in succession performances of this work with Giulini and the Vienna Philharmonic Orchestra, and was convinced that I could never listen to this music being played by anybody else. A few years later Evgeny Fyodorovich convinced me of the opposite. Now it is even difficult for me to describe what exactly it was that so impressed me in Svetlanov's reading of this symphony: it was simply unbelievably fresh and talented, and very individual, without the slightest hint of any 'originality'.

I cannot fail to remember one moment that had no direct connection to music, but, as soon became clear, was a very significant one. After that concert one of the musicians asked me what I thought about Svetlanov's performance, mentioning its 'untraditional nature'; his tone in saying this, incidentally, indicated that 'untraditional nature' here meant debatable, inadequate, incongruous. Yes, Svetlanov's interpretation was really very individual – but there was nothing in it that in the least degree contradicted the spirit and letter of Brahms! And in me arose the involuntary suspicion: do all the musicians of the State Orchestra realise what lucky people they are, *who* was leading them? You get used to good things and, probably, even to the work of a genius.

The attitude of some members of Svetlanov's orchestra towards their leader over many years was, let us say, peculiar. When I was still a child discussions were held about my possible performances with Svetlanov, and someone from the State Orchestra administration decided to warn my teacher, Anna Pavlovna Kantor: 'In one rehearsal Zhenya will discover the whole alphabet!', meaning by this what in our time is called 'unprintable language'. What can I say? During the entire period of my relationship with Evgeny Fyodorovich and our work together *not once* did I hear from him a single swear word or even merely a rude one. When, at one of our rehearsals together of Beethoven's 'Emperor' Concerto, a member of the woodwind section played something quite different from what was in the music, Evgeny Fyodorovich, in a perfectly calm tone, said, 'Actually it's time to know this music, it has already existed for several centuries. Although,' he added, 'as Nikolay Pavlovich Anosov* would have said, "it has a certain 'refreshando".'† What kind of alphabet was this?! Clearly Svetlanov, from a family of the Russian intelligentsia, understood perfectly which words and expressions should be used and when, and he made use of them appropriately.

But once the following happened. During that same rehearsal of Beethoven's 'Emperor' Concerto, when we had played it right through and Evgeny Fyodorovich asked whether everything suited me, I requested that

---

* Nikolay Pavlovich Anosov (1900–1962), conductor, composer, pianist, father of the conductor Gennady Rozhdestvensky.
† 'refreshando', a parody on Italian words used in classical music to indicate tempo, character and emotional colours.

he speed up the tempi in the first and third movements, because he had taken very restrained tempi which were not what I felt to be best. At first Evgeny Fyodorovich was surprised. During a break he sat on the platform conducting something to himself, but then, when the rehearsal resumed, he began to conduct at my tempi, which clearly he had tried to understand and fully feel during the break. It seemed to be fine, but later I heard from an acquaintance, the wife of one of the players in the orchestra, that at that moment the orchestra had split into two: one side was indignant that Kissin had dared to ask the maestro to change something, the other did not share that indignation. Hearing this I thought ye-es, it is probably only in Russia, with its centuries-old traditions of deference, that such a crazy situation could arise!

What happened between Svetlanov and the State Orchestra in the years before his death is well known. It was a difficult time then, in the 1990s: the musicians were in urgent need of payment, and their main conductor, in demand throughout the world, could not supply them with it. All this is understandable, but what is striking is the solution the State Orchestra chose to this situation: simply breaking relations with Svetlanov, once and for all depriving themselves of creative contact with a great conductor, thanks to whom this group had become one of the best orchestras in the world! I also do not understand how those who a few years earlier had been indignant 'that Kissin dared to ask for something from Svetlanov' could allow what ensued to happen, if they worshipped their maestro to such a degree?!

In principle, such an attitude of orchestral players to a conductor of genius is nothing new. In Herbert von Karajan's time, shortly before his death, there arose a conflict with the Berlin Philharmonic Orchestra, which he had conducted for forty-four years. There, naturally, it was not a matter of the musicians' pay, for they had money coming out of their ears, but of something quite different: they had become spoilt. Karajan decided to take into the orchestra the outstanding clarinettist Sabine Meyer, who later became a famous soloist and to this day enjoys the well-deserved recognition of music lovers. But this contradicted the 'good old' tradition of the Berlin Philharmonic, according to which only men could play in it! The maestro did not take into account the sexist protests of his musicians, who became very angry with him and stubbornly continued as such right up to the end of his life. Incidentally, shortly after Karajan had created this 'outrageous precedent', they began to accept women into the orchestra without any objections. Now there are very many representatives of the fair sex in the Berlin Philharmonic – and nothing happened; for some reason the orchestra did not begin to play worse as a result!

As for the State Orchestra, shortly after their break with Svetlanov their new administrator came specially to St Petersburg, where I was then giving concerts, and asked to meet me, announcing the following: 'I must tell you openly: now, after we stopped working with Svetlanov, we have problems, so we need well-known soloists, and we want to ask you to perform with us.' It is simply interesting – what were they, after all, counting on when they drove out Svetlanov? At the time I gave no definite reply; I think that this man understood me, because no more invitations came from the State Orchestra. Naturally, I have no desire to make music with such people.

The last time I heard Evgeny Fyodorovich in London, not long before his death, he performed Rachmaninov's Second Symphony and only words like 'masterpiece' and 'miracle' can be applied to describe that concert. To this day there rings in my ears the main theme of the first movement: anxious, with the most refined rubato, each note in it speaking, each of the constantly changing harmonies being brought to the audience in all their beauty. And the third movement . . . Svetlanov generally liked slow tempi, like many musicians who have a lot to say, and so it was that he took a very slow tempo – and a true revelation was the result.

One of the dearest mementoes in my home is a letter from Evgeny Fyodorovich which I received a few weeks before he left this world. In it the maestro responded very flatteringly to one of my recordings which I had sent him not long before his death ('Now that was a present!') and expressed the wish, which became for me a kind of testament, that I should play Medtner. As is well known, Evgeny Fyodorovich loved Medtner very much, and tried to make his music better known. Shortly after the death of the maestro, remembering his behest, I learned and included in my repertoire Medtner's Sonata-Reminiscenza.

The Proms

One of the most memorable recitals of my life, which thanks to YouTube became available to millions of listeners, was at the Proms in London's Albert Hall in 1997. There is always a special, very democratic atmosphere at this festival, and regardless of the fact that the hall was not designed for classical concerts, to play at the Proms is a great pleasure. My first appearance was before I left Russia. I played Tchaikovsky's First Piano Concerto, and then, a few years later, came an invitation to give a solo recital. In all the history of the Proms (which date back to 1895) they had never arranged piano recitals, and so on the one hand I was extremely flattered, on the other I doubted how a piano would sound in a hall holding six thousand listeners? Even when there are large symphony orchestras, the sound does not really fill the hall. I went there to try the piano on the platform and, yes, there was not much sound, not enough to fill the hall . . . And suddenly one of the people present had an idea: what if the piano were not on the platform, but in the centre of the hall? The fact is that the Albert Hall is a sort of arena where there is an inactive fountain, and around it during concerts stand listeners who do not have money for more expensive tickets. They decided to try it, placing the piano in the arena behind the fountain – and it sounded incomparably better. Before my recital they erected a raised platform for the piano and stool behind the fountain.

On the day of the recital it was very hot in London and I had a cold, but I played successfully, and I am very glad that the greater part of the recital, including seven encores, was recorded on video and has become available to many listeners. It was at this very time that Christopher Nupen, the outstanding film director and creator of many films about music and remarkable musicians, made a documentary about me. He filmed my solo recital at the Proms, and the second part of the film consists exclusively of the pieces played at the request of the audience, who would not let me go (and they still say 'cold-blooded Englishmen'!); the seven encores, together with applause, lasted about forty minutes.

Talisman

Approximately a year after our move to New York I became acquainted with Arthur Rubinstein's widow,

Aniela. At the end of 1992 she was in that city and wanted to meet me. At our meeting were also present their daughters Eva and Alina. Aniela turned out to be a very kind woman, and later I visited her home in Paris several times. A month after our meeting, I took part in an orchestral concert in Carnegie Hall; going into the green room before the concert, I saw a package on the table. In it was a handkerchief on which were embroidered the initials AR, with a sprig and the date 1973, and also a letter from Rubinstein's eldest daughter Eva, who wrote something like this: 'When my father was alive my mother and I sewed him handkerchiefs with his initials which he wore in the breast pocket of his jacket at all his concerts. I want to present you with the handkerchief that I embroidered for Daddy in 1973, when you were still very small, because you are the only pianist whose playing reminds me of my father.'

Since that time I too wear this handkerchief in the breast pocket of my jacket at all my concerts. I have now had this talisman for over twenty years.

Part III

VARIA

'Ikh bin a Yid'

Once, in childhood, I wrote the following testament (at that time, naturally, I could not imagine that I would live anywhere other than Russia):

'When I die, bury me in the region around Moscow, in the forest, and let the stone, under which my remains will lie, be barely visible in the grass and [it] should look like . . .' – going on to draw an oblong with the following inscription above the dates of my life:

HERE LIES EVGENY KISSIN,
SON OF THE JEWISH PEOPLE,
A SERVANT OF MUSIC

And a few years later I read in Aitmatov the legend of the mankurts, and thought that if I had to find myself in such a situation and if they put on my freshly shaved head a hot piece of camel skin, I would constantly repeat aloud the words, 'Ikh bin a Yid' ('I am a Jew', in Yiddish) – so that even after I had forgotten who I was and what I was, these words would remain on my lips.

As a child I spent the summer at the dacha with my grandma and grandpa and heard them speak in Yiddish a lot. Since those distant days something has remained in my soul . . . and when I grew up, there arose in me a wish to learn this language properly, which I gradually did over a period of many years. Then I began, in so far as my modest powers allowed, to promote Yiddish poetry, reading in public poems in Yiddish, and even recorded a number of compact discs of Yiddish poetry.

It would seem obviously silly to judge and, even more, to make public pronouncements about things that you do not know – and yet, some far from silly people do it. I well remember how at the end of the 1990s, after a scandalously anti-Semitic speech by Makashov, *Literaturnaya gazeta* published, under the headline 'The Jewish Question – a Jewish Response', two articles, one of which was written by Dmitry Bykov. In his 'Jewish response', Dmitry L'vovich announced, among other things, that the heights of culture were only achieved by Jews who had been assimilated into other cultures, but 'to call Sholem Aleichem a genius – forgive me, parochialism is parochialism'. Well, Sholem Aleichem, thank G-d, has long ago firmly entered history, the best judge, as a great writer, and Bykov's opinion cannot change anything. As for Hebrew literature in general, Bunin, for example (and his stern attitude to other writers, even to Dostoyevsky and Chekhov, is well known) did not consider it below him to translate into Russian Mendele Mocher Sforim; Akhmatova – Markish, Galkin and Kvitko; Khodasevich published a whole book of his translation of Hebrew poetry, and Chukovsky referred to Sholem Asch in the highest terms (incidentally, contrasting him with Jewish writers who pursued careers in Russian literature, without creating anything of worth). What is more, two Jewish writers, Shmuel Agnon and Isaak Bashevis Singer were even awarded the Nobel Prize in Literature: to put it mildly, it is clear that people who work in the Nobel committee are no less competent than Bykov. I am concerned that the readers of *Literaturnaya gazeta*, or at least the majority of them, are probably not aware of these facts, and have not read these writers and poets, and could therefore easily believe the nonsense that supposedly the heights of art have only been reached by Jews who had been assimilated into other cultures, and that Jewish literature is parochial. And in any case, far from all the masterpieces of Jewish literature have been translated into Russian, especially poetry. The Russian reader is hardly likely to be familiar with such names as Jacob Glatstein, Leyvik, Aaron Tseytlin, Itzik Manger, Kadia Molodovsky, Rakhil Korn and many others, with whose work I was only able to acquaint myself through knowledge of Yiddish.

Or, for instance, an article written some years ago by Mikhail Veller under a heading borrowed from Lenin, 'Critical remarks on national question': it is clear that the author does not know Yiddish, for instance of 'az okh un vei' he writes 'azokhenvei' – but quite categorically calls this richest and most expressive language 'pidgin German'!

And very recently I read an interview with Leonid Parfenov, held in connection with the appearance of his new film about Russian Jews, in which he says with conviction that he, as the film's *auteur*, was concerned with 'Jews who wrote in Russian, leaving us more serious literature than that which is written in Yiddish'. For anyone who is familiar with Yiddish literature it is clear that such things can only be said by a person who is not acquainted with it – but why talk about something you do not know?

I therefore try, so far as I am able, to acquaint people who do not read Yiddish with the great poetry created in this language. From my teenage years I have loved poetry, loved reciting it, and I think that many years of reading experience have developed my taste in literature and my ability to understand it. Yiddish poetry is great poetry, belonging to the highest achievements of world culture; and it is only possible to create such poetry in an exceptionally rich and expressive language that possesses immense inner strength and is capable of conveying the subtlest thoughts and feelings.

At one time I conceived the desire to translate into Yiddish my favourite Russian songs: 'A Little Song about White Bears', 'A Song about Hares', 'Dark Nights', 'Moscow Windows', 'About a Wood Deer', Vysotsky's 'Ballad of Struggle' and several others. By that time I had already met and become friendly with the Jewish writer Boris Sandler, who for many years worked as chief editor of the oldest Yiddish newspaper in the world, *Forverts*, which is published in New York. I started to send my translations to Sandler, and he willingly edited them. And finally I began to write my own texts in Yiddish: verse at first, and later prose too. Sandler did not approve of my first attempts to write poetry, but about the third one he said, 'it is already poetry' and edited it; the poem was about how my granny and grandad at the dacha talked to each other in Yiddish and I, as a child, listened and asked what this or that word meant, and how those few Yiddish words have remained in my memory and soul my whole life . . . Of course, I always knew feelings such as inspiration and spiritual trepidation while playing the piano, but I shall never forget how, in the middle of the night in Paris, I went to the kitchen and experienced those feelings when some lines of poetry came into my head, or, rather, soul:

Mayne zeyde Arn, bobe Rokhl,
mayne libe, zikhroynom-livrokhe,
mayne tayere, mayn glik un vey –
okh, vi s'vilt zikh hofn mir un gloybm,
vos atsind zey zeen dort, fun oybm,
vi ikh shrayb af yidish vegn zey!

My grandad Aron and granny Rakhil,
my beloveds, blessed be their memory,
my dear ones, my happiness and pain –
oh, how I want to hope and believe,
that now they see, there up above,
how I am writing about them in Yiddish!

After this I continued to write poems on various themes and Sandler began to edit them and publish them in a special blog on the site of *Forverts*. And a few years ago I was drawn into an epistolary polemic with a certain woman on the interesting topic of marital infidelity. In this quarrel I spoke from a liberal position, suggesting that infidelity is not always bad, and managed partly to convince my opponent, who suddenly shared with me the thought that had come into her head under the influence of our polemic: 'You know, one may be unfaithful even for the sake of love: let us say your husband has been put in prison, and the only way to save him is to sleep with somebody in authority.' Then she also wrote that, for the same reason, 'you could also work as a prostitute', and then I thought that this would be a good subject for a short story. For a long time I was convinced that I was not capable of writing such a story myself, but the subject continued to pursue me – and finally I decided to do it. Sandler liked the story, edited it and published it in the print version of *Forverts*. Since then I have written several short stories, and I am now writing a novella in which I fantasise on the following theme: into our family, instead of my sister Allochka (that is, ten and a half years before me), was born a boy who was the exact opposite of me in character, physical features, interests and so on. The only thing we had in common was that we both loved Yiddish. When I read the first chapter to Sandler he said, 'Continue in the same spirit!', so with the blessing of my literary teacher I am proceeding with enthusiasm.

There Are Always Good People Everywhere

Sometimes they were even found amongst the guards in Nazi concentration camps.

I have known well what anti-Semitism is from early childhood. In the house in which I lived the first thirteen and a half years of my life there were only two Jewish families, us and our neighbours the Shapiros – and the majority of children in our house were aware that I was a Jew, and frequently reminded me of it. I had to suffer a lot because of this in our yard, not, incidentally, only from children, but also from one of the adults. I have not previously told of this publicly, and I do not want to go into details because I do not wish to look like a victim 'begging for pity', but in a book of reminiscences it is impossible to remain completely silent about these facts, otherwise the story of my life would be incomplete and even, in a way, distorted.

Despite all this, I have never for a moment had the smallest thought or feeling that being a Jew was bad. I remember Mother once talking to me on this theme, recalling various great people who had been Jews. What is more, we have preserved at home a little paper that was given to me after my debut with Chopin's two concertos in Moscow; on the paper was printed a poem. Its essence for me was, of course, not in its poetic merits but in . . . let us remember: the year 1984, the dead period of 'stagnation', when state anti-Semitism was flourishing, and amongst the people the very word 'Jew' was perceived as slightly indecent and better avoided. And suddenly, at this very time, somebody hands me, a twelve-year-old boy, the following poem:

To Zhenya Kissin

Having discovered art and nature,
They were always persecuted by fate.
Praise to the Jewish people!
I bow down before them!
For their patience, minds and customs,
For their unbending attitude to work,
For the genius which is rightly born
In their righteous Jewish environment!
And now to the world has been announced
By the hand of a Jewish boy

That a new genius, having become an idol,
Has stridden into future centuries!

Valentin Khoprov

I remember this and each time tears come to my eyes.

And then again there was our school . . . Amazing details come to mind now: for instance, at one of the physics lessons Lyudmila Valentinovna Kostina suddenly mentioned that Hitler made exterminating the Jews one of the aims of his life! And our teacher of harmony, Inna Evgenevna Shchelkunova . . . oh, what a remarkable woman she was: clever, sharp-tongued but always just, and if somebody deserved commendation (both as a pupil and simply for some human act), then Inna Evgenevna always praised them and was truly overjoyed. And so, one day during one of her lessons, Inna Evgenevna suddenly for some reason started to talk about the Jewish cemetery in Prague. One of my classmates at the time made a remark to the effect that there were 'no crosses there'. And to this day the voice of Inna Evgenevna rings in my ears pronouncing these words: 'There are never any crosses in Jewish cemeteries.'

'This above all: to thine own self be true'*

When, a few years ago, I yet again watched the 1977 film *Office Romance*, I suddenly heard in one of the songs words to which I had never before paid any attention and which now shook me so much that I wanted to learn them by heart and write them down:

Let the walls of your house be fragile,
Let all roads lead to darkness,
There is no betrayal sadder on earth,
Than betrayal of yourself.

How exact, how merciless – and how true. After all, it is like the words of Rabbi Zusya of Annopol: 'When I die, the Almighty will not ask me why in times of difficulty was I not Abraham or Moses: he will ask why I was not Zusya'!

My good friend Lord Weidenfeld, now deceased, used to say he had three elements of self-identification: he grew up in Austrian culture, spent most of his life in England and was a convinced supporter of European democracy and, being a Jew, identified himself with the Jewish people and the state of Israel. I could say something similar about myself: I grew up in Russian

---

* Shakespeare, *Hamlet*, Act 1, Scene 3; Polonius's parting words to his son Laertes.

culture, all my conscious life I have been a convinced European and at the same time from childhood felt myself unambiguously a Jew. As I have already said, when in 2002, retaining my Russian passport, I became a British citizen, it greatly simplified my nomadic life. But at a certain moment I began to feel that, for my soul, something was missing. I am very grateful to Britain for the fact that she took me into her family, and I feel great respect for this, the oldest democracy in the world, a country that gave humanity Shakespeare, Newton, Watt, Jenner, Stephenson, Faraday, Darwin, Churchill . . . but, if I may say so, what sort of an Englishman am I? And so, following the calling of my soul, several years ago I turned to the Israeli government with a request for Israeli citizenship. In my letter of request, I wrote in particular: 'I always deeply despised chauvinism and never considered that my people were higher than other peoples. I consider it a real blessing that my profession is probably the most international in the world; that I play music created by great composers of various countries; that I travel throughout the world and share my favourite music with people of different countries and nationalities. But I want all people who value my art to know that I am a Jew, that I belong to the people of Israel. For that reason I feel a natural desire to travel around the world with an Israeli passport.'

My request was granted: now I do indeed travel with an Israeli passport, and for me that is far more natural than presenting a British one. I have lived in many countries and do not know whether I shall ever come to live in Israel, but I feel towards that country, compared with other countries, the same sentiment that was accurately expressed by Mayakovsky in his poem *Very good!*:

> I have seen places where figs and quince
> grew without difficulty near my mouth.
> One has a different attitude to such places.
> But the earth, which I had won
> and, half-alive, nursed to health,
> where you arise with a bullet, and go to bed with a rifle,
> where as a drop you pour into the masses –
> with such a land you will go to life,
> to labour, to festivity, to death!

Of course, in a direct sense I did not have to win Israel, or nurse it, but over the last few years I have constantly published on my sites material about what is really happening in that country; I often come across various prejudices on this subject which are very widespread. Perhaps this sounds too much, but now I really feel myself a soldier of Israel on an international front.

Russia, the West, Israel . . . There is, however, yet another country which is dear to my heart and I shall write about it separately.

Georgia

Once, in an English journal in which there was an article about me, for some reason I was described as a 'Georgian pianist'. It brought to mind what Charlie Chaplin said when asked whether he was a Jew: 'I am not a Jew, but I do not have anything against people considering me a Jew.' So it is with me: though I am not a Georgian, I have absolutely nothing against being considered a son of this remarkable people. Of course, objectively, good and bad peoples do not exist, but each nation has its peculiarities, its temperament. As the convinced internationalist Aleksandr Bovin said in one of his interviews, 'To me, for example, Jews are nicer than Arabs, Americans than Germans, the Chinese than the Japanese.' I personally am not capable of thinking badly of any nation in the world (from childhood I have felt ethnic hatred directed towards me, and I know well what a foul thing that is), but there are peoples that are closer to my heart than others – and Georgians are especially close to me. Practically every time I meet a Georgian, there arises an immediate contact, a special inner closeness.

Strange as it is now to remember, the first time I went to Georgia, at the end of March 1988, it was unwillingly and with apprehension. The administration of our school insisted on a visit to Georgia to an All-Union Congress of Music Schools, as a result of which I had to put off a visit to Poland planned for the same time – Poland, a country of which I had dreamed all my life: the native land of Chopin! And I was apprehensive because of the idea widespread in Russia (and not only there) that 'in Georgia they love Stalin'. It is true that at that time, in crowded Russian cinemas, they were showing as often as they could *Repentance*, the anti-Stalinist film by the Georgian Tengiz Abuladze, but I, like many others, still thought that not everyone in Georgia shared the position of the *auteurs* of this film. As for their supposed love of Stalin, on the first evening of my stay in Tbilisi I became convinced that it was just one of many stereotypes which so harm the relationships between peoples.

Immediately on arriving in Georgia Anna Pavlovna and I were taken to a flat owned by people we did not know who accepted us as their own and took good care of us throughout our stay in Tbilisi, and also during my second visit to Georgia a year and a half later: that was the Charkviani family. The head of the house, Georgy Georgievich, felt in us 'his own people', and on the very first day started to speak at table about politics from an anti-Soviet position, normal at that time. When Anna Pavlovna hinted that we might visit such a place of note as Gori, the village where Stalin was born, Georgy Georgievich replied, 'Oh no! There is nothing to look at there: a fanciful little house' – and it became clear that there was no whiff of Stalinism here. And later the elderly uncle of our hostess, Elena Dmitrievna, visited the house, and in spontaneous conversation about religion suddenly said, 'And those people told us there is no God! Stalin is your God! And with him Beria, Yezhov . . .' and so no doubts remained on this question. This man later continued his political disquisitions, and in the end produced a classic Menshevik–Sukhanov thesis: 'What did Marx say? That a socialist revolution is possible in a developed capitalist country. That means that in an undeveloped country it is impossible. But they went on and abused great Marx! And here are the results!'

Later it was very comic: this old boy asked me what my name was.

'Kissin,' I said.

'A typical Russian surname. And what is her name?' – he indicated Anna Pavlovna.

'Kantor,' I replied.

'What, is she a German?'

Our hosts' daughter, Marianna (with whom I later became very good friends) quietly replied: 'Well, a German name . . .'

The old man fell silent and in a significant tone stated: 'Young man, you have a classical appearance: you look like a Russian and a Georgian and a German!'

Well, it was very pleasant to hear, of course.

From that very first visit to Georgia I fell fully in love with the country, its people, Tbilisi. What I felt then may be described in the words used in her time by Veriko Anjaparidze to Solomon Mikhoels in farewell when the Moscow State Jewish Theatre was leaving Georgia after a tour: 'Tbilisi is not merely a city. It is a heart.'* And I also felt, and always feel to this day, what Veriko Ivlianovna said to the widow of Mikhoels after his murder: 'The meeting with Mikhoels was sent to me by heaven as confirmation of the meeting between two peoples – Georgians and Jews.'

Those who hate my people like to put forward the following argument: since, they say, everyone, everywhere disliked the Jews – that means there must have been a reason. A clear example that refutes this assertion is wonderful Georgia, where Jews have lived for 2,600 years, and over all that time there has not been a single pogrom! Of course, there is no family without a freak, and in any people there exist black sheep – but, as is well known, the exception always proves the rule. When, in the wild 1990s, somebody defaced several graves in the Tbilisi Jewish cemetery, the President of Georgia, Eduard Shevardnadze, personally sent a guard to the cemetery, saying that 'we shall not allow anyone to attempt to destroy the centuries-old friendship between our peoples'; and when, at approximately the same time, some wretched small newspaper in Georgia published an anti-Semitic article, Shevardnadze made

---

* Cited from the book by Matvei Geizer, *Mikhoels*.

an announcement along these lines: if it happens again, we shall close the newspaper.

I myself always felt personally the attitude of Georgians to Jews. It consists of such subtleties that many of them cannot be described in words, and so I shall give just one example. When perestroika began, it was in Georgia that for the first time in the Soviet Union there began official, permitted courses of Hebrew, and when this happened my new Georgian friends said to me, a Jew living in Moscow: 'We will go and learn Hebrew, and then teach you!'

And from my very first visit to Georgia I was delighted and inspired by its general spirit of internationalism. In a certain sense the incarnation of this was that same Charkviani family. I know, although I did not question them about details, that with a predominance of Georgian blood, they also have Russian, Jewish and other blood as well. Again, in all peoples there are some swine, including chauvinists, and my Georgian friends told me about such people, but for myself I always saw and felt in all the Georgians with whom I was lucky enough to become friends, or simply to talk to, a real spirit of internationalism. Many in Russia like to speak of the 'genocide of Ossetians' in South Ossetia in August 2008, and at the same time they do not want to know that after that war they not only expelled all Georgians, whose ancestors had lived there for centuries (as had happened in Abkhazia sixteen years earlier), but that also thousands of Ossetians, whose ancestors had likewise settled there for hundreds of years, of their own free will escaped to Georgia, as did Russians, Ukrainians, Jews, Estonians and others, and at that time not one Ossetian was expelled from Georgia, not one Abkhazian, not one Russian, nobody! In a book that my Georgian friends had once given me I found a poem, the like of which – with perhaps the exception of Lessing's play *Nathan der Weise* – I had not found in all world literature (I have in mind of course real, great literature). This poem was written about a century ago by a Georgian national poet who was by origin an Armenian, Ietim Gurji:

Man, love equally
the Georgian and the Jew,
for we are living and growing older
and on us sinners
death has been looking for a long while
with its pair of infernal eyes.
Man, love equally
the Armenian and the Ossetian.
If we cannot love
and protect each other,
believe the prophet Ietim:
they should shave us off like bristle,
they should singe us like bristle,
like despised bristle,
off the face of the Earth!

In these lines, for me, is the whole of Georgia, the blessed, beautiful Georgia . . .

At the end of the 1980s, when many peoples of the Soviet Empire began to struggle for independence, it was obvious to me from the very beginning that such a struggle was just and had to be supported. At the time I became involved in the problems of Georgia, and after the bloody dispersal of a peaceful meeting in support of the independence of Georgia on Rustaveli Avenue in Tbilisi on 9 April 1989 I wrote a poem:

Kartveli! O, most unfortunate people!
Blood pours from a gaping wound.
As soon as a free southern spring breaks through the
    ground,
a northern avalanche covers it . . .
Let he who lies be accursed forever,
blaming you for giving us a tyrant
you, whom he himself renounced,
whom he subjected to persecution!
Now we must bow down to you
and stand up for justice together, alongside, level.
The empire is cracking at the seams!
but from beneath the seams spurt fountains of
    blood . . .

---

* *Kartveli* means Georgians.

When, several months later, I gave an interview for the television programme *Before and After Midnight* and its presenter, Vladimir Molchanov, asked me which of the speeches at the recent Congress of Peoples' Deputies had made the greatest impression of all, I expressed my indignation at the speech of General Rodionov, who was in charge of the massacre of 9 April, in which he not only tried to justify, but, one might say, strongly defended the bloody crime that had been committed under his leadership. A little while later, I was on tour in Tbilisi and people stopped me in the street and thanked me: 'You are a good man!'

Georgia, my beloved, I am always with you.

Am I a Romantic?

I am quite often asked whether I consider myself a romantic musician. But does it not seem after all silly to say of oneself, 'I am a romantic'? However, a very nice young man whom I got to know soon after moving to America said precisely that, entirely seriously, loudly and with a broad smile. And nonetheless I replied as I think: as a man I have a romantic nature, and this naturally comes out in my music. Voinovich, in his book *A Portrait Against the Background of Myth*, writes of himself in his youth: 'I was far from remote from romantic impulses, although I did not like this myself and tried to squeeze romanticism from myself drop by drop, like a slave."* He was trying to squeeze it out, while I, on the contrary, am trying not to lose that element of myself; it would hinder Voinovich in his work as a realist writer, but for me it is the opposite, helpful and essential, otherwise I should cease to be myself. Sviatoslav Richter, a typical representative of the intellectual tendency in musical performance, used to say that it was harder to play romantic than classical music, because classical music could only be played with the intellect, whereas for romanticism feelings were necessary. Heaven forbid, I do not compare myself with anyone, but remembering that statement of Richter's, I cannot help thinking that for me personally, from childhood, it was easier to play romantic music than classical, precisely because romantic music needs feeling!

There is another interesting example: in my teenage years I recall reading in a book on Aleksey Nasedkin his words about how early on he loved sculpture, dramatic plays and prose, and considerably later on came to love poetry and painting. I, by contrast, in my childhood loved poetry and painting more than anything. And all the above-mentioned forms of art I came to love considerably later; apparently this was because Nasedkin was a musician of an intellectual bent, and I of a romantic one. All the same, Evgeny Yakovlevich Lieberman,

---

* Voinovich is referring here to Chekov's words, known by every Russian: 'All my life I have been squeezing the slave out of myself drop by drop.'

whom I mentioned earlier, in a review of my debut with Chopin's two concertos, quoted the words of Heine that Chopin should be considered a Hellenist, and wrote that my art was rather classical than romantic – in the same sense as Chopin's. I remember that this was the only place in Evgeny Yakovlevich's review that surprised Anna Pavlovna, and with which she did not agree. However, I understand why he wrote as he did. After all, it is not for nothing that Chopin, who has remained in history as a shining representative of the romantic movement in music, himself did not like romanticism! And such an ingrained romantic as Sofronitsky was absolutely right when he wrote (I quote from memory): 'Chopin was the most chaste and strict of all the romantics. He must be played with great spirituality and at the same time boldly and simply.' A few years ago such thoughts started to come into my head: are classicism and romanticism really the only tendencies in music? Can musical performers really be divided into 'intellectual classicists' and 'emotional romantics'?

The Sublime

When, at the first Tchaikovsky Piano Competition in Moscow, Van Cliburn won outright, Aleksandr Borisovich Goldenweiser, one of the most distinguished professors of the Moscow Conservatoire at the time, characterised the playing of this utterly romantic pianist thus: 'This boy, when he plays, is talking to God.' You certainly cannot say that of all romantics; at the heart of romanticism undoubtedly lies an emotional core, but emotionality and *the sublime*, emotionality and *inspiration* – these are different things. And Furtwängler, by the way, how could you characterise him: 'romantic', 'classicist' or, perhaps, 'universal'? Hindemith wrote that Furtwängler transformed musical experiences into religious revelations. It is interesting that my teacher Anna Pavlovna, a person very far in her life from religion and religiosity, often said to me during our lessons when I was small and playing that same Chopin, and not only Chopin: 'And here you should pray.' The great Carlo Maria Giulini, in my opinion, was a representative of precisely such a direction in art – call it what you will: neither romanticism nor classicism, but depth, sublimity and spirituality. He, incidentally, was a man of deep faith – but in this case it seems to me that it is completely unnecessary: one can be an unbeliever or not adhere to any of the traditional religions, but at the same time possess a natural and strong feeling of the sublime and the divine, and express this feeling in one's art. And that is what has always been for me the closest thing of all.

The Earthly

Here, of course, I should make the proviso that I naturally always played music such as, for instance,

Shostakovich's First Piano Concerto without any kind of spirituality and sublimity, for there is not a trace of them there. As the Leningrad professor Natan Efimovich Perelman said absolutely accurately in his splendid book about playing the piano, 'Serious performance of unserious music is as inappropriate as unserious performance of serious music.' When many years ago I played Shostakovich's First Piano Concerto in Salzburg (that was on the eve of my first meeting with Karajan), a local reviewer praised me, contrasting me with other pianists who, in her words, 'make of this deeply sad composition some kind of clownery'. Of course she was exaggerating: there is no sadness in the last two movements of this concerto, much less deep sadness; but in the second movement it is definitely present, and the first movement, in my opinion, is far more than simple 'clownery'. Furtwängler was inclined to dramatise even undramatic music. Once again, I do not compare myself with anyone, but I too always did this and still do.

De Gustibus

I was at a concert – or, more accurately, at the open rehearsal that was, in essence, the first concert – of Vladimir Horowitz in Moscow in April 1986, and it seemed to me, like many other Muscovite listeners, that for all his stunning pianistic virtuosity he had bad taste, which was especially apparent in Mozart's C major Sonata. I remember similar responses from musicians and music lovers to Horowitz's playing after his performances in the Great Hall of the Conservatoire: 'Well, I don't know: his Scarlatti was fine, but when he got to Mozart the trickery began.' 'He plays like a ballroom pianist of genius. In my opinion, he simply played the Mozart sonata badly.' And at that time I reacted to Horowitz's playing similarly. On this subject I shall say what, in my view, is the difference between Mozart in the hands of Horowitz and, for instance, in those of Samuil Feinberg, who also played Mozart with great rhythmical freedom and whose recordings of Mozart I like very much; it is, in my opinion, the very thing about which Sofronitsky was talking when he commented on Horowitz's performance of Chopin's mazurkas: 'Cortot makes rubato twice as much as he, and it sounds tortuous, but it is never sweet.'

The concept of bad taste has differed at different times, something, incidentally, to which Harold Schonberg gives much consideration in his book *The Great Pianists*, noting that previously a sign of bad taste in a musical performance was an inadequate quantity of rubato, dryness of playing. However in his fine book about Horowitz even Schonberg writes that at the beginning of the 1980s, when for reasons of health and age Horowitz began to play worse, 'some of his mannerisms started approaching bad taste'.

*

Here it is probably worth saying something about my attitude to Horowitz's art in general. I remember how, when Richter's *Diaries* were published, some readers (*not* musicians) could not understand why Richter did not like Horowitz. Some people argued that Tolstoy did not like Shakespeare, and so what? But in fact, if you read attentively what Richter said about Horowitz, then it becomes clear that Richter did not 'dislike' Horowitz, but reacted to him *equivocally*: ' . . . both phenomenal and outrageous, both super (in Conservatoire manner), and wonderful sound, and nonetheless inconsistent. What a talent! And what vulgarity . . . So attractive, artistic, and so shallow (listen to his laughter and look at him).' Just so: both one and the other. I personally agree with almost all Richter's evaluations of various musical recordings in his *Diaries*, and my attitude to Horowitz generally always corresponded to Richter's: something in his performance aroused my huge admiration, and yet there was something truly alien. Alien to me was that Horowitz was and has remained in the history of pianistic art above all a Virtuoso, with a capital letter, great, unique – but all the same mainly and precisely a Virtuoso. For me the most important thing in music, in the art of performance, has always been not virtuosity but something quite different, something that I wrote about earlier. Therefore when, after my first concerts in America, certain enthusiastic critics started to compare me with Horowitz, and even to call me the 'new Horowitz', intelligent musicians understood that in reality such parallels were false and only made because in America Horowitz was considered pianist no. 1, and therefore were the highest compliment to me, but did not reflect at all the way I was playing. I always felt closer to such pianists as Dinu Lipatti, Heinrich and Stanislav Neuhaus and the young Cliburn; and, of those who did not make great careers but were musicians I respected and loved – our unforgettable 'Gnessin Patriarch', Teodor Davidovich Gutman. But of course much of Horowitz's heritage cannot fail to arouse my admiration: his sonatas by Scarlatti, Clementi and Haydn, and many of his recordings of music by Chopin and Rachmaninov, and Schumann's *Kreisleriana*, and of course Liszt and various virtuoso pieces, and Horowitz's own arrangements – in these, it seems to me, he had no equal.

Gilels

From fairly early days Anna Pavlovna began to think about the question of who I would continue my musical education with after leaving school, and up to October 1985 she wanted, when the time came, to 'hand me over' to Emil Grigoryevich Gilels. A few years later, our acquaintance Liya Moiseyevna Levinson, the well-known pianist and teacher (a marvellous woman who for many years was the assistant of A. B. Goldenweiser), and a close friend of Gilels and his family, told us that Gilels's widow had conveyed to her the words of her husband shortly before his death: 'The only person I should like to teach is Kissin.'

I remember that morning in October 1985 when Gilels passed away in the restaurant of a Budapest hotel (that was the time of so-called 'days of Soviet culture in Hungary' in which I was taking part). At breakfast the pianist Evgeny Mikhailovich Shenderovich said, 'It is very sad about Emil Grigoryevich,' and I, a boy of fourteen, having already absorbed the Soviet mentality, thought, 'Has he really *emigrated*?!' Later, it seems on the same day, Spivakov told me, then I first heard from the lips of Vladimir Teodorovich what very many now write in Russia: 'Gilels was a great musician, but in our country he was put down by comparison with Richter: they made of Richter a deity and lowered Gilels to just "a great artist".'

And when nowadays people ask who I think is better, Gilels or Richter, I reply that, personally, I feel closer to Gilels, but I do not say that he was better; they were both great musicians. In reality it seems to me that Gilels and Richter are essentially musicians of a similar type, but Gilels is closer to me because, unlike Richter, he had a quality that is dear and important for me, namely emotional warmth. And that is how it has been all my life from childhood. To this day the face of Gilels stands before my eyes and I hear in my ears fragments from the first variation and finale of Schumann's *Études symphoniques*, as he played them at a recital in the Great Hall of the Moscow Conservatoire, which was broadcast on television when Andropov died. What depth in every note! Well, and Gilels's live recording of Beethoven's 'Hammerklavier' from a concert in the Great Hall of the Conservatoire, which took place less than a year before his death – that in my opinion is the peak of performing art. Once again: what unbelievable depth, range and inner strength! And in the reprise of the third movement, in the passage of transition – this is true passion, deep and tragic. One can only inwardly bow one's head before such a genius.

Amongst Living Pianists

Closest to me are Martha Argerich and Grigory Sokolov. In my opinion, the recording by Argerich of Schumann's *Kreisleriana* is one of the greatest of all. And I like Martha very much as a person: she is so sincere, direct! And how modest: she has reached such heights in art, and to this day during rehearsals asks musicians present in the hall (some of them not fit to hold a candle to her) for their opinion about her playing. We have several times played duets – and what a pleasure it was for me, not only as a musician, but also on a purely personal level. We live in different countries and therefore do not talk often, but every time we meet some spiritual currents flow between us. She is a wonderful woman.

I highly esteem some recordings by Vladimir Ashkenazy, for example, of Chopin's Second Sonata, Beethoven's Seventeenth, Brahms's First Piano Concerto, Liszt's Transcendental Études, a compact disc with Rachmaninov's Third Piano Concerto and five Preludes issued to mark Rachmaninov's centenary. I also highly esteem such pianists as Murray Perahia, András Schiff and Krystian Zimerman. I cannot fail to mention the recording of Bach's Goldberg Variations performed by Daniel Barenboim. Once I watched a video of Glenn Gould playing the Goldberg Variations (his last recording) and for many years was convinced that nobody could ever reach such a level, and therefore there was no sense in playing this work at all; but when I heard Barenboim's recording, then I once again became convinced: *in art there is no end and cannot be one.*

Of pianists who have not made great careers and are therefore less well known, I very much like Richard Goode: it seems to me that his recording of Beethoven's Twenty-Eighth Sonata is unsurpassed. I remember being at one of his recitals in a private house in New York, and when he began to play Beethoven's Twenty-Fifth Sonata, and the arpeggios on the first page (D major, B minor and one V56 [first inversion of the 7th chord] leading to A major), each of them with its own colouring, a man sitting behind me exclaimed 'Ah!' at each arpeggio.

In Words about Music

Within the piano repertoire there is, as is well known, not much programme music. Of course, sometimes composers themselves have written a 'programme' to some of their works: for example, Tchaikovsky to his Fourth Symphony (in a letter to Nadezhda von Meck), Scriabin to his Third, Fourth and Fifth Sonatas. In some cases familiarity with the history of musical works affords the possibility of better understanding their content. For instance, the full image of Medtner's Sonata-Reminiscenza came to me after I had learned how it had been created: the Civil War, a cold and hungry winter, a forest in which stood the house of one of the friends of the Medtner couple. And Nikolay Karlovich himself, peeling potatoes with his valuable fingers – the only food they had. Reading all this, I imagined that the Sonata-Reminiscenza was nostalgia for the old world disappearing forever in the flames of the Civil War.

Nearly fifteen years ago I played Medtner's sonata in various countries, and it was simply amazing how everywhere my audiences loved this hitherto unfamiliar music, how it penetrated to their very hearts. By the way, the same thing occurred a few years earlier with 'The Lark' by Glinka/Balakirev, which I used to play as an encore. And it happened a few years ago with Scriabin's Second Sonata and his Études opus 8:

hardly anybody in the West knows this music, and they all come to love it very much! What a good thing it is that I was born and grew up in Russia, in this culture, with this music – and now I can share it with the whole world.

But some works inspire me to make my own 'programme', or even texts to the music. Of course that is my own fantasy, but all the same I think that it does not contradict the spirit of the music. For instance, as soon as I began to learn Sergey Prokoviev's Sixth Sonata (I was not yet fourteen), I immediately imagined that the main theme of the first movement was the image of Stalin. By that time the above-mentioned Viktor Yuryevich Dashevsky, my history teacher, had already explained to me that Stalin was a tyrant and a murderer. And about ten years ago, while rehearsing Brahms's Second Piano Concerto in Toulouse, suddenly there arose in my head a text in Yiddish to the music of the orchestral introduction to the third movement. Returning to my hotel after the rehearsal, I finished composing it and wrote it down. It sounds as follows:

From high heaven quietly can be heard the voices of angels . . . How beautiful! They sang about the L-rd and His world, about our life and its sorrows, about happiness and about love . . . Brahms had heard them and immediately noted down their beautiful melody, in order that people should hear it and preserve it forever in their hearts. Blessed be you L-rd, our G-d, king of the universe!

When I play Brahms's First Piano Concerto, I think about the Book of Esther. The very beginning, the threatening first theme, is Haman's decree throughout the Persian Empire to destroy the Jews. Later, when the eerie theme played softly by strings begins and gives you goose pimples – that is the horror that seizes the Jews. The second movement is an image of the beautiful Esther. And the third movement is the Jews assembling and rising up in defence of their lives. The fugato in the middle represents groups of Jews gathering from various places for the battle. The long cadential 46 before the cadenza means it is all over, the battle is finished and the Jews have won. The cadenza that follows in which the major gradually comes to the fore describes the Jews realising that all the danger is past, that they are saved. And in the coda to part of the triumphant theme I sing to myself, 'We are alive! We are alive!'

Moreover, some circumstances of my own life have occasionally inspired me to certain associations. When I was nine and lived with my granny and grandad at the dacha, I often pined for my mummy and daddy, who could only come there on their days off. And one day, when Mummy and Daddy were departing, I played the first movement of Beethoven's Twenty-Sixth Sonata, which has the subtitle 'Les adieux', then for the rest of the week I played to myself the second movement ('L'absence'), and when my parents returned I played the third movement ('Le retour').

And in the finale of Schubert's D major Sonata I see the image of an old, kind Viennese Jewish watchmaker, much loved by children, to whom he sings, 'Come to me, little children and I will tell you a story and sing you a little song . . .'. In the G major episode he tells of his beloved daughter and at the very end of it sings, 'Oh, dear daughter! Oh, dear daughter! I love you so much!'

I remember that when I first played 'The Two Jews' from Musorgsky's *Pictures from an Exhibition* to Anna Pavlovna, she said to me: 'Well, the rich Jew in your version is a scoundrel! And a rat, too!' And when I play this piece now, I think of the passage from Sholem Aleichem's novel *Tevye the Dairyman*, where Aronchik's rich uncle says to Tevye, 'You should not forget who you are and who we are. How can you even think that Tevye the milkman, who brings us cheese and butter, could be our relative? Well, don't imagine you will be able to make a scandal, to trumpet everywhere that my nephew was wooing the daughter of Tevye the milkman! And get out of your head the idea that my sister is someone money can be squeezed out of!'

Chopin's Seventeenth Étude arouses in me images from Voloshin's poem 'At the Circus': the beginning and end of the work remind me of

The clown in a fiery circle . . .
The crude and cruel laughter is like leprosy,
and on his gypsum-like face
two eyes burning with pain

And in the middle of the Étude I recall the words of Voloshin in his poem:

> By the light of the moon
> he sings at his window
> A song of swan's passion
> to Columbine and the moon.

And when, as a teenager, I played Rachmaninov's Étude-Tableau in E flat minor from opus 39, I said to myself that it was Russia in 1917 as well as 1917 in Russia (this work was actually written in 1917). The second movement and the second theme of the Finale of Rachmaninov's Second Piano Concerto with its oriental colouring I always associate with the great Russian poet Esenin's Persian cycle.

When a couple of years ago I began to study the Arietta from Beethoven's Thirty-Second Piano Sonata, I immediately had the thought, or, rather, feeling, that it was the greatest thing in the world of psychotherapy! How this music lifts us up above all the sorrows and petty problems of life.

Several years ago I became acquainted with the psychologist and writer Vladimir Levi. We talked for a while and Vladimir L'vovich asked me to play something on his piano, so that he could record it on tape to remember me by. And I decided then to play the finale of Schubert's Sonata in E flat major, because I felt that in this music there was exactly the mood in which you leave a good psychotherapist! This music is so kind, full of light and tenderness . . . Sofronitsky was right when he said, 'Nobody possessed such an amazing soul as Schubert.'

I also have some unusual ideas about Saint-Saëns's Second Piano Concerto, especially its finale, and about Prokofiev's G minor Gavotte from his opus 12 – but I do not want to talk about these works in advance, before I play them: let it be a surprise for my audience!

Returning to Rachmaninov . . . I remember that Anna Pavlovna, when I was still a teenager and just beginning to play his music, used to say that Rachmaninov's broad, melodious themes were the breadth of Russian nature. Since then I always feel this strongly, although when playing Rachmaninov's lyrical music I do not imagine Russian landscapes visually, but simply experience the emotions that they arouse in my soul.

Recently I remembered that as a youth I read Esenin's poem 'My Beloved Land!' and immediately fell in love with it; not only did I not attempt to imagine before my eyes Esenin's visual images –

'ricks of sunlight in the bosom of the waters.'

'On the boundary where flip over the mignonette and the chasuble of the clover. And the willows, like modest nuns, ring their rosaries. The marsh smokes with a cloud, burning in the heavenly yoke.'

– but I didn't even think of the meaning of all these words. I was seized by Esenin's emotions at the nature of the beloved land that he described: 'With a quiet secret for someone I have concealed my thoughts in my heart. I keep meeting everything, accepting everything. I am glad and happy to remove my heart', and suddenly there is the terrible and prophetic, 'I have come to this earth in order to leave it rather soon.'

In my work I do not approach music from musicological positions. The intellectual task for me consists in making the performance sound well and organic; in preventing the structure from falling apart, in avoiding halts, seams, superfluous little endings; if the composer writes a lot of forte or a lot of piano, one must avoid it sounding monotonous; how to distribute the balance between hands and various voices; how to avoid uniformity of rubato and so on. Or here is another example: when I was studying Medtner's Sonata-Reminiscenza, Anna Pavlovna, hearing me from another room, once said to me, 'In this sonata there are many different lyrical themes: think how to make them all sound differently.'

In other words, I see my task as being to use my intellect for the maximum emotional effect of the music on the audience.

Chopin's Polonaises

In the summer of 1985 I learnt Chopin's Polonaise in F sharp minor. Anna Pavlovna was immediately pleased with the way I interpreted this music, which was very close to her, and after several months I first played the polonaise publicly at the 'December Evenings' festival. Later Anna Pavlovna said that other listeners had commented on my playing as follows: 'Unusually powerful, and, generally speaking, strange.' Elena Somoilovna Ephrussi said, 'Now people consider that there is only one way of playing! This is a dreadful age!' But I, for my part, did not at the time understand what seemed strange in my performance. Now I do. For me that polonaise is full of drama and tragedy; that is how I instinctively responded to it when I was thirteen, and that is how I hear it now. In my childhood and youth I suffered from a nervous tick, and once, after I had played this polonaise again to Anna Pavlovna, I began to twitch so much from my feelings that Anna Pavlovna said it was probably not worth my playing it because it had a bad effect on my nervous system. The accepted way of playing it was different, without any tragedy, and even not especially dramatically, more like an austere dance. When I learned it I associated it with *Mtsyri*, and the mazurka in the middle with the lines about a beautiful young Georgian woman.* Later I understood that this polonaise was about the tragedy of Poland, Chopin's native land, enslaved and ravished by the Russian Empire; that the episode before the mazurka is the approaching army (after all, you can literally hear drums and trumpets!), and the mazurka itself is the image of Poland, a beautiful Polish girl. And at the very beginning of the polonaise are signs of the cross: of course, Poland's case was for Chopin sacred. To this day I do not doubt that it was precisely this meaning that Chopin gave to his Polonaise in F sharp minor – this is so completely evident to my ears, so obvious to me. And only many years later did I learn that the next polonaise, in A flat major, Chopin wrote when in the grip of his feelings after the battle near Grochów in which the Poles crushed the Russian army. I do not think this is by accident: the Fifth Polonaise is about the defeat and tragedy of his fatherland, and the Sixth concerns a small, local event, but nonetheless a victory.

Chopin . . . Chopin

Here something very interesting happened in my life. I began my path on a large stage with Chopin, and

---

* *Mtsyri* is the title of a romantic narrative poem by Mikhail Lermontov (1814–41) about the experiences of a novice who runs away from his monastery.

Chopin's music has always from the very beginning occupied a central place in my repertoire; but until recent times, to the question 'Who is your favourite composer?' I always replied sincerely that I was an omnivorous person and could not choose – not only a single favourite composer, but not even two or three, although I placed above all other composers Bach. Over many years I felt that Beethoven was not in the least less close to me than Chopin, but that I needed a great deal of time to play the music of Beethoven on, let us say, an adequate level, in order to feel myself freely in it as a performer. From this I drew the conclusion that love of music and the ability to play it well are not one and the same thing, and that the one far from always coincides with the other. Once I made for myself a conditional list of five of my favourite composers on the principle of the number or even percentage of their compositions that were close to me: they were Bach, Mozart, Beethoven, Chopin and Brahms. But recently I have begun to feel ever less close to Brahms, with the exception of certain of his works, for example, the Third Violin Sonata, which I have always adored after having heard it played by Vladimir Spivakov when I was not yet thirteen; on the other hand, for the first time in my life I felt that there was, after all, one composer whose music was closer to me than the others: it was Chopin.

With the Years I Become More and More Aware

Life is full of contradictions and it is constantly necessary to make sacrifices, but in one aspect of my life, in concert performances, I have understood or rather felt this for a long time. Always, from my childhood, I have loved to play before an audience, but at the same time, alas, I cannot do it too often because concert performances exhaust me – not so much physically as emotionally. Twice I tried to give solo recitals with only a day in between, and each time the second recital turned out worse; one day was not enough to restore myself, to 'fill myself up' after the previous recital. For that reason the greatest number of concerts I have ever played in the course of one year (1993) was fifty-six. But generally, as a rule, I give between forty and fifty concerts a year. Recently I have been feeling that I am not as young and strong as I was twenty or even ten years ago, and so I prefer breaks of three days between recitals. It is much simpler when playing with an orchestra in that you play far less, and so, accordingly, I can play with an orchestra two or three days running, as is customary.

I have to plan my concerts two to three years before the date, because the timetables of concert halls are established well ahead. But the programmes, luckily, do not have to be planned so long before: at most a year, and often even less. I could never understand why the administrators of concert halls do not like the same pieces to be played during a particular concert season; it seems to me that, on the contrary, it would be interesting for the public to hear the same work treated by different performers! But, nevertheless, that is how it is.

For concert days I had a regular regime for many years. In the morning I spent a couple of hours rehearsing in the hall. I took lunch, lay down for two to three hours in bed, where sometimes I managed to fall asleep, more often not, but all the same it is important to relax and rest. I returned to the hall an hour and a half before the start of the concert, and for forty-five to fifty minutes I warmed up on the platform. But as of late, on the day of the concert I simply sleep in, then I rest and come to the hall to warm up immediately before the concert. And after the concert I have dinner and then for a long time cannot fall asleep: even sleeping pills do not help . . .

Modesty

How is it possible for us performing musicians not to be modest when we are constantly, many hours a day, in touch with great music, the level of which we shall never reach!

People not infrequently send me their compositions and ask me to play them. One young man from Brazil sent me his works, announcing in the accompanying letter the following: 'I hope that you will promote my music in the way that Arthur Rubinstein promoted the music of Manuel de Falla.' And so I look through such 'creations', and each time I am struck: after all, these people know the music of Bach, Mozart, Beethoven, Schubert, Chopin . . . well then, how can they not realise how talentless and insignificant is what they themselves write? Or do they so want to write that it simply does not come into their heads to make comparisons?

I personally never plan to bring this or another work onto the platform unless I am sure that I can perform it at a sufficiently high level to make it worthy of comparison with the already existing interpretations of the music. Another matter, of course, is that I am far from always achieving this. It sometimes happens that on stage my performance is successful, but not in recording studios; my live recordings are as a rule better than those made in the studio. And there are some works which I shall never study – I know, for example, that I shall never play Ravel's 'Scarbo' like Samson François in his first recording of this work, or the Goldberg Variations like Gould and Barenboim. So what right, it might be asked, do I have to take up the valuable time of my listeners? And Richter was absolutely correct when he confessed in his memoirs that he did not even begin work on Brahms's First Piano Concerto and Prokofiev's Third Piano Sonata because he knew that he would never be able to play them as well as Gilels. That is an example of the attitude of a real, great, self-critical artist.

And when people ask me what my task is as a performing musician, I always reply that in my view it is to become as close as possible to what we are performing. Of course only the greatest of the great can reach this level, but we must strive our utmost to come close to it.

Never Say 'Never'

After this book was first written something began to happen in my life that contradicted the thoughts expressed in the previous section: I began more and more to compose music.

As I have mentioned, in childhood I wrote a lot of music. Beginning at the age of two to play by ear, I soon started to improvise, and when I went to school and learned musical notation, I immediately began to write down my own music. At first I wrote for the piano, later also for other instruments and for the voice. I tried out several instruments, various styles – and at a certain moment felt that my own music stopped sounding in my head. I was about fourteen then and was beginning an active concert career, and then for many years thought that once these things coincided – that was how it was meant to be: the purpose of my life was not to compose music but to play the piano. But suddenly, a few years ago, something unexpected began to happen. At first, when at night I lay in bed tortured by insomnia, various musical ideas suddenly started to come into my head – as a rule it was combinations of various chords which relaxed me. Then some ideas also began to come to me in daytime; in particular more than once there returned to me the thought of the possibility of writing a dodecaphonic tango, and in my ears I could hear its rough outline. A little while later I wanted to finish a toccata for piano that had been begun in 1986 and for some reason left unfinished. Altogether I wrote a cycle of four piano pieces ('Meditation', 'Dodecaphonic tango', 'Intermezzo' and 'Toccata'). Well aware of the phenomenon of graphomania, and also that sufferers from it are themselves unaware of it, I asked for a meeting to be arranged for me with the composer Arvo Pärt, who in those days was in Paris. I showed Arvo Avgustovich my attempts at composition and asked him, 'Please tell me honestly, is it worthwhile my continuing with this or not?' – and I received the reply that it was undoubtedly worthwhile. Pärt also gave some absolutely good advice about 'Meditation', to which after our meeting I immediately made some appropriate corrections.

The support of such an authoritative composer as Pärt inspired me, and I continued to write: for voice with piano, for string quartet, later for cello and piano. I started to send my compositions for comment (in no way requesting that they be performed) to various esteemed musicians with the unchanging request: 'Please give me your honest opinion; if you consider that it is bad, just tell me, and I shall not be in the least offended,' and I not only received very flattering responses from the majority of my addressees, but some of them even began to play my music! Well, I am not counting on anything and have no pretensions, I do not in the least overestimate the achievements of my compositions – I simply do not resist inspiration and continue to compose. Let us see what comes of it and how audiences will respond to my music.

For All My Deep Respect towards Heinrich Neuhaus

I cannot agree with his statement that the best performer of a musical work is by definition its composer. And not only does it come down to the fact that far from all composers possess sufficient technique to perform their own works; there is another important point.

When we were still living in Moscow, Anna Pavlovna told me that Rachmaninov recorded his Third Piano Concerto at such swift tempi because at that time there were no long-playing records and long works simply did not fit onto records. But many years later, having already moved to America, I read in the memoirs of Rachmaninov himself that the Third Piano Concerto lasts thirty-three minutes: that means that Rachmaninov really thought of the work like that. But at such a fast speed it is not possible to say everything that is placed in this music, to express all its depth, drama and tragic feeling. And then I began to think: did great creators always fully realise *what* they had created? And was, for instance, Scarlatti being coquettish when he declared in the first edition of his piano sonatas that these pieces were trifles and contained nothing? He probably really did not consciously put into, say, the music of his B minor Sonata what many centuries later Gilels heard in it. Incidentally, when Tatyana Nikolayeva first played Shostakovich's Preludes and Fugues, Dmitry Dmitrievich, hearing her performance, said, 'I did not know I had written such good music.'

I have an old friend from Tbilisi, a professional composer who has already been mentioned, a very serious and educated person, Marianna Charkviani. Once, during one of our conversations about music, she unexpectedly uttered a thought which I had myself had earlier without telling her: 'A composer is a medium.'

In this context there arises an eternal question for us performing musicians: what should be the attitude of a performer to the composer's text? I personally agree with Anton Rubinstein, who said, 'First play everything exactly as it is written. If after that you feel like changing something – then do it.' As a rule, I try conscientiously to fulfil all the composer's indications, but sometimes, as everyone knows, it happens that in certain places it is simply impossible: it sounds bad and unnatural. Yes, even the great, when composing music, cannot always hear in every detail how it will 'actually' sound; it is probably for this very reason, as we know from recordings, that certain great composers (Debussy and Rachmaninov, for instance) sometimes did not follow their own indications when performing their compositions.

I received unexpected confirmation of this from a story told by the above-mentioned pianist and professor Dmitry Aleksandrovich Bashkirov, heard recently in a broadcast by Sati Spivakova from the television series *Classics That Are Not Dull*. This story was known to Bashkirov from his teacher Goldenweiser, who in his youth was friendly with Rachmaninov. Shortly after the first performance of Rachmaninov's Second Concerto, played by the composer himself, Goldenweiser had to play this concerto and asked Rachmaninov to accompany him on a second piano.

They begin to play, but on the second page Rachmaninov stops and says to Goldenweiser: 'It is too fast.'

They play on. Soon Sergey Vasilevich again stops and says: 'It is too slow.'

They continue to play. A few pages later Rachmaninov says: 'It is too loud.'

They play a little more and Rachmaninov says: 'It is too quiet.'

Finally Aleksandr Borisovich says, imploringly:

'Sergey Vasilich, but I am playing everything as it is written!'

Rachmaninov says: 'What does it matter what I wrote there!'

Sometimes, in rare cases, I allow myself to depart from the composer's directions in certain details, if it seems that it sounds better that way and does not contradict the spirit of the music. For instance, in the last episode of the finale of Schubert's D major Piano Sonata, at the time of the rise to high A I do not make a crescendo but a diminuendo. I do the same in the last piano reprise in the second movement of Brahms's First Piano Concerto: not crescendo but diminuendo in the rise to high B flat. In that way the music arouses in me even greater veneration, and in my view it will have the same effect on the listeners too.

In general, it seems to me that all this was said with complete justification by that same N. E. Perelman in his above-mentioned book of aphorisms: 'In interpretation there is one limit: distortion.'

Inspiration

In childhood, when I had just begun to appear before the public, it sometimes happened that, when going onto the platform, I was not inspired and in the right mood, and the whole recital felt lacklustre.

And so, when I was fifteen and was touring in Japan

with the 'Moscow Virtuosi', in the first half of the concert in Tokyo I played Mozart's Twelfth Piano Concerto poorly, but in the second half, Shostakovich's First Piano Concerto turned out well. After the concert Spivakov came into my hotel room and asked, 'What happened in the Mozart?' I replied that I had not been in the right mood, whereupon Vladimir Teodorovich gave me a 'lecture' which helped me greatly. 'A true artist should create his own mood,' said Spivakov. 'Do you think it was easy for me to play a Mozart concerto with Bernstein in Salzburg? Do you know how nervous I was? But I constantly repeated to myself how wonderful it was that I was playing in Mozart's city with Bernstein himself, what happiness . . . and then I was called back onto the platform seven times after the quiet ending of the concerto! And if I had given into a "mood", you can imagine what I would have brought down on my head there!'

Not immediately, but gradually I too have learned this. For the rest of my life.

Soon after my move to New York I was invited to perform at the Radio City Music Hall at the Grammy awards ceremony. I had to play, for about three minutes, the last part of Liszt's 'Spanish Rhapsody'. They then gave me a room with a piano to warm up in, there was plenty of time, I played and played, repeating it . . . and after my performance, which was broadcast live around the world and watched by 1,600,000,000(!) viewers, the representative of BMG Classics who was accompanying me said, 'You looked so calm!' And on that occasion I learned that the more you practise, the better you play; you feel more calm and self-confident. And this discovery has served me well throughout my life. Then I understood that two things are necessary to cope with pre-concert nerves: to prepare thoroughly for the concert and from the very beginning, before even coming onto the platform, to immerse yourself in the music.

In the first years of my life and active concert activity in the West, during the concerts I used sometimes to have a feeling of routine. One day in spring 1994, performing in the Italian city of Bologna, I went onto the platform to play a recital with such a feeling but nonetheless I played well, my performance clearly pleased the public, and after I had performed four prepared encores, they simply would not let me leave the platform! I came onto the platform again and again, but the public continued to applaud with ever-increasing enthusiasm. Well, I played from memory something else as an encore, but the listeners continued to demand more and more! I began to play various encores . . . and finally, after the thirteenth encore, when the time was half past midnight, firemen came onto the platform and announced, 'This theatre is a municipal building, and therefore we are closing!' – only then did the applause fall silent. And I was in seventh heaven, and felt ashamed that at the beginning I had come out onto the platform to play the recital without inspiration.

And a few years later I was in Cologne and played Beethoven's Second Piano Concerto with the local orchestra under Rudolf Barshai. One day, between the rehearsals, I had time to spare and went for a walk along a pedestrian street in the city centre and suddenly I heard music. I went closer and saw that four musicians in the street were playing a Beethoven quartet (moreover, all except the cellist were standing), and on the ground lay a case for people to throw money in. These musicians, playing for passers-by, few of whom even paid attention to them and stopped to listen, were not only of a high professional standard, but played with such immense commitment, with such inspiration, that at that moment and forever after I became ashamed and asked myself how I could sometimes go onto the platform and play for people who had paid money and come to listen to me without full engagement. And from that time, although of course not all concerts can be equally successful, each concert has for me been an event, and at every concert I give everything I have.

What a remarkable musician Rudolf Borisovich was, and how interesting it was to work with him. At that time I was playing Beethoven's Second Piano Concerto for the second time in my life. I remember how we went through this concerto together to the last episode of the second movement, where there is a kind of dialogue between piano and orchestra, and the orchestra plays part of the main theme pianissimo. Barshai at first said this is 'a conversation with the heavens', and then asked me, 'And how do you think, should this be played intensely or simply very quietly?' And then he advised me not to slow the tempo before the reprise in the third movement and, in particular, said, 'Shostakovich would not have slowed the tempo here' (Barshai knew Shostakovich well). And later I understood that in reality it is better not to slow the tempo at that point. Generally, it is sometimes better for the achievement of greater effect *not* to stress things. Both in music and in life.

And Rudolf Borisovich also told me that Shostakovich began every working day by sitting at the piano and playing Bach; and quoted the words of Shostakovich that music should be composed in the way that Bach did it; it is not important in what key, and on which instrument you play, it will sound well all the same. And it is really true! But who, apart from Bach, could do it?

On Fame

What can I say . . .? Never in my life have I striven for fame, and in my youth I even found it a painful burden, but one thing it gave me is very important and valuable: the possibility to meet and get to know outstanding and remarkable people. Thanks to the fact that in my time I was awarded the Triumph Prize, I met such writers as Vasily Aksenov, Andrey Voznesensky and Vladimir Voinovich. I am eternally grateful to fate for bringing me together with Elie Wiesel, whom I deeply venerated. Shortly after reading Ilya Gililov's *The Shakespeare Game: The Mystery of the Great Phoenix*, mentioned earlier, which became one of the strongest impressions of my life, I had the possibility of meeting and later becoming a friend of the author, an utterly remarkable man.

And, of course, there was Vladimir Bukovsky, whom I revered like very few other people in history, when, shortly after our arrival in America, I read his books *To Build a Castle* and *Letters of a Russian Traveller*; a few years ago fate granted me the opportunity to meet and talk with this great man. And through Bukovsky I got to know Garry Kasparov.

One of my dreams was not fated to come true. Early on I dreamed of making the acquaintance of the actor and clown Yury Nikulin and accompanying him – not, of course, in a public performance, but in some intimate friendly company, my favourite 'Song about Hares'. Alas, I was not in time. Granted, it sometimes happens in life that the thing you dream of does not come about, but on the other hand the thing that you do not dare to dream of is given to you by fate.

When, about ten years ago I, for the only time in my

life, consulted an astrologist (she was our neighbour on the landing of our London flat), she, having made my chart, said to me, amongst other things: 'Of your ten planets seven are in the air and not one on the earth, and for that therefore you are not in the least interested in material things, but ideas interest you, and you like interesting people who supply you with ideas.' I should never have been able to describe my own character so accurately. And this really came about . . . well, if not in childhood, definitely since my youth. I remember when we were staying at Ivanovo, the Composers' Home in the country (at that time I was fifteen), my mother, worried that, as it seemed to her, I was not mixing enough with my contemporaries, would say to me, 'Well, go to the other young people! Otherwise you are with one old man or another all the time.' In reality I frequently did mix with the young people there, but it is true that it was more interesting for me to be with the 'old men'. (Oh, and what old boys there were at Ivanovo! That is a separate story: perhaps I shall tell of these unforgettable people in another book.) And at that time I already did not feel in the least like a child.

In my childhood and youth I was so shy that I simply felt physical discomfort when unknown people recognised me in the street. Gradually I learned how to react to this calmly, and in recent times I have begun to catch myself even feeling pleased when people recognise me and say something good about my playing. Although, when at the concerts of my colleagues people ask for my autograph, especially on concert programmes, that is very stressful for me to this day.

Feedback

As for admirers of both sexes, if they are normal people, why not? With some of them I have even become friends and am very glad about it, because they turned out to be good people. Unfortunately, amongst admirers there are not a few 'special' people, something that I have encountered frequently in my life, and I have found it far from easy: alas, this too, if I could put it that way, is the cost of our profession. I keep interesting correspondence from my listeners, and I have a special packet in which I put letters that go beyond normal bounds, for instance, from women on the theme 'I want to have your child,' 'I want to give you my virginity,' 'if you are Schumann, I want to be your Clara,' and suchlike. Once I showed a few of these letters to a close friend of mine who, though not a psychiatrist, is a doctor and possesses a great store of knowledge in various fields of medicine; he simply made psychiatric diagnoses of them one after another.

And sometimes it befalls me to receive simply unbelievably comic letters from listeners. One day, for example, there came from New York a letter along these lines:

A few months ago I handed you a cassette with a recording of three piano sonatas by Hindemith, and expected, at least, a thank-you letter, but since I have received nothing so far, please send the cassette back and I shall give it to somebody more grateful: my father, for instance. And what is more, in my youth I often attended the Marlboro Chamber Music Festival organized by Rudolf Serkin, but I only managed to exchange a few words with him; and I have often been to the recitals of Arthur Rubinstein and Vladimir Horowitz in Carnegie Hall, but afterwards they were always surrounded by a crowd of people, and so I simply could not speak even a word to them; and after your last recital in the Carnegie Hall a black woman in the green room [that was the adorable Debbie King, who works behind the scenes in Carnegie Hall and always and very touchingly looks after the musicians performing there] would not let people approach you. I do not know why we hero-worship some people; it seems we are all equal. In general, I want my tape back.

To which I replied:

Sir, I thanked you when you gave me the tape, and do not consider that I should have sent you a thank-you letter as well. Of course I shall return the tape to you, but unfortunately you will have to wait, since I have left it in New York and am myself now in Europe and shall only return to New York in a few months' time.

After a while I received another letter from this man:

Mr Kissin, I must apologize: the fact is that just before I wrote you my first letter the girl I was dating left me and for that I reason I was in a very bad mood, so keep the tape, and in general you are a good man.

And once a letter came to me from Ireland with the following content:

Mr Kissin, I am a great admirer and enjoyed your last recital in Dublin until the moment at the beginning of the Brahms sonata when I heard that the high E flat had gone out of tune, and after that I shuddered, waiting for the next E flat and so on until the end of the recital. I rang the hall's administration and asked why they had not retuned the E flat, to which I received the reply that if the musician did not ask for it, they had no right to interfere. Therefore I want to ask you two questions: 1) if it really was your responsibility, why did you not ask them to retune that note? 2) do you think it is fair to expect a paying audience to sit through such an experience?

I replied to this gentleman that I had not heard anything of the kind, because I only listen to the music, and not to individual notes, and do not think that any one of us can speak for all listeners, but if he considered that he had been cheated, I was prepared to return half the price of the ticket to him: for the second half during which I played the Brahms sonata. A couple of years later I again came to Dublin, and there they told me, 'Do you know, some person has sued us for the fact that during your recital some note went out of tune! The case came to court, this man tried to question the qualifications of the concert organisers . . . well, the judge realised who he was dealing with and his application was rejected.'

In general, for several decades I have often recalled the advice that was once given me by Lazar, the son of the Armenian artist Martiros Saryan. At that time, when I was still a schoolboy, I was performing with the 'Moscow Virtuosi' orchestra in Yerevan, and there was such a sell-out crush that before the start of the concert they would not let me into the hall; they did not know that I was performing, and took me for a young person trying to get in without a ticket. The next day after the concert Lazar Martirosovich took us around Armenia, showed us the wonderful ancient churches of Garni and Gehard, and Anna Pavlovna told him what had happened the previous evening. Then kind Lazar Martirosovich gave me, a twelve-year-old, some parting advice: 'Zhenya, the main thing is do not lose your sense of humour. He does not let you in and shouts, but you say to him calmly, "I need to go in." He, "A-a-a!". And you say calmly, "I am telling you that I need to go in." He, "A-a-a!". You say calmly as before, "Well, I am telling you that I need to go in . . .", and then somebody comes up and explains that you are a performer and so on. But if you become angry and yourself start to shout, "A-a-a, scandal, I am a performer!" that will mean that you have simply lost your sense of humour!'

Happily, the majority of letters I receive from admirers are very pleasant and touching. What is more, many of them are really very important to me, because they answer a question which I have always over many years asked myself and the reply to which is generally for me the most significant thing in life: why do people need the thing to which I have devoted and am devoting my life? All these nuances, subtleties on which we work every day throughout our lives, striving to reach a certain goal – why do people need all this? And various people from different countries and over many years have written and continue to write to me how my music has helped them to cope with serious existential problems such as illnesses, and thank me for that. And to such people I unfailingly reply, 'You cannot imagine how important to me is a letter such as yours. Thank you for it.'

Credo

It is surprising how sometimes people you hardly know can play such an important role in your life. Over several decades a man called Yakov Mikhailovich Rubinstein taught history in our school. I studied in the same class as his granddaughter Natasha, and I think it was for exactly that reason I did not get to study with him: probably he did not want to teach his own granddaughter, and therefore retired when the time came for our class to study history. I personally hardly knew Yakov Mikhailovich, and it seemed that we spoke briefly only once or twice (I remember how, after our leaving revue, at which our class performed a potpourri on various themes assembled and arranged by me, Yakov Mikhailovich came up to me and said, 'I liked the way you had first the "Internationale", then "Hava Nagila" and then "Glory to the Russian people"!'), but several of my acquaintances and friends, former pupils of our school, told me what an exceptional man and teacher he was; what truly encyclopaedic knowledge and wisdom he possessed, and of the love and respect that he constantly attracted from his pupils.

And one day (and this happened a month and a half before Yakov Mikhailovich's death: he died a few days before reaching ninety-nine), while reflecting on certain issues that were worrying me, there arose in my head one historical-existential question to which I could not give myself an answer. And I decided to put this question, through Natasha, to Yakov Mikhailovich, whom, I repeat, I practically did not know. The reply I received became for me a kind of testament from this amazing man – and my credo for all of life. It deserves to be printed in capital letters and to form the end of this book:

AT ALL TIMES AND IN ALL SITUATIONS, REGARDLESS OF SEX, AGE AND CREED, FOR INTELLIGENT PEOPLE (AND ESPECIALLY FOR THE JEWISH INTELLIGENTSIA) MOST VALUABLE OF ALL HAS BEEN AND REMAINS HUMAN LIFE.

Select Discography

Audio Albums

JAMES LEVINE – LIVE AT CARNEGIE HALL
Works by Wagner – Beethoven – Schubert
BEETHOVEN, Piano Concerto No.4 in G Major, Op.58
BEETHOVEN, Rage Over a Lost Penny: Rondo a Capriccio in G major, Op. 129
Yevgeny Kissin
The MET Orchestra
Int. Release 24 Mar. 2014

EVGENY KISSIN – FANTASY
Works by J.S. Bach – Beethoven – Brahms – Gluck – Liszt – Schubert – Tchaikovsky
Berliner Philharmoniker
Herbert von Karajan, Conductor
Claudio Abbado, Conductor
Int. Release 02 Mar. 2007

FRÉDÉRIC CHOPIN
[1] Polonaise in C-Sharp Minor Op.26 No.1
[2] Polonaise in E-Flat Minor Op.26 No.2

[3] Impromptu in A-Flat Major Op.29 No.1

[4] Impromptu in F-Sharp Major Op.36

[5] Impromptu in G-Flat Major Op.51

[6] Fantaisie-Impromptu in C-Sharp Minor Op.66

[7] Polonaise in C Minor Op.40 No.2

[8] Polonaise in A-Flat Major Op.53

Evgeny Kissin, Piano

(P) 2006 Sony BMG Music Entertainment

FRANZ SCHUBERT

[1] Fantasie in F Minor for Piano Four Hands D.940

[2] Allegro 'Lebensstürme' in A Minor for Piano Four Hands D.947

Evgeny Kissin and James Levine, Piano

Recorded live May 1, 2005, Carnegie Hall, New York City

(P) 2006 Sony Music Entertainment

FRANZ SCHUBERT

Sonata 'Grand Duo' in C for Piano Four Hands D.812

[1] Allegro moderato

[2] Andante

[3] Scherzo – Allegro vivace

[4] Allegro vivace

[5] Characteristic March No.1 in C D.968b

[6] Military March No.1 in D D.733

Evgeny Kissin and James Levine, Piano

Recorded live May 1, 2005, Carnegie Hall, New York City

(P) 2006 Sony Music Entertainment

ALEXANDER SCRIABIN
Five Preludes Op.15
[1] No.1: Andante
[2] No.2: Vivo
[3] No.3: Allegro Assai
[4] No.4: Andantino
[5] No.5: Andante
Sonata No.3 in F-Sharp Minor Op.23
[6] Drammatico
[7] Allegretto
[8] Andante
[9] Presto con fuoco
NICOLAI MEDTNER
[10] Sonata – Reminiscenza in A Minor Op.38 No.1
IGOR STRAVINSKY
Petrouchka: Three Movements
[11] No.1: Danse russe
[12] No.2: Chez Petrouchka
[13] No.3: La semaine grasse
Evgeny Kissin, Piano
(P) 2005 Sony BMG Music Entertainment

FRANZ SCHUBERT
Sonata in B-Flat D.960
[1] Molto moderato
[2] Andante sostenuto

[3] Scherzo – Allegro vivace con delicatezza
[4] Allegro, ma non troppo
FRANZ SCHUBERT / FRANZ LISZT
[5] Ständchen (From Schwanengesang D.957)
[6] Das Wandern (From Die schöne Müllerin D.795)
[7] Wohin? (From Die schöne Müllerin D.795)
[8] Aufenthalt (From Schwanengesang D.957)
FRANZ LISZT
Mephisto Waltz No.1 S514
Evgeny Kissin, Piano
(P) 2004 BMG Music

JOHANNES BRAHMS
Sonata in F Minor Op.5
[1] Allegro maestoso
[2] Andante espressivo
[3] Scherzo: Allegro energico
[4] Intermezzo: Andante molto
[5] Finale: Allegro moderato ma rubato
[6] Intermezzo in A Minor Op.76 No.7
[7] Capriccio in B Minor Op.76 No.2
Five Hungarian Dances
[8] No.1 in G Minor
[9] No.3 in F
[10] No.2 in D Minor
[11] No.7 in F
[12] No.6 in D-Flat
Evgeny Kissin, Piano

(P) 2003 BMG Music

FRÉDÉRIC CHOPIN
24 Preludes Op.28
[1] Prelude No.1 in C
[2] Prelude No.2 in A Minor
[3] Prelude No.3 in G
[4] Prelude No.4 in E Minor
[5] Prelude No.5 in D
[6] Prelude No.6 in B Minor
[7] Prelude No.7 in A
[8] Prelude No.8 in F-Sharp Minor
[9] Prelude No.9 in E
[10] Prelude No.10 in C-Sharp Minor
[11] Prelude No.11 in B
[12] Prelude No.12 in G-Sharp Minor
[13] Prelude No.13 in F-Sharp
[14] Prelude No.14 in E-Flat Minor
[15] Prelude No.15 in D-Flat
[16] Prelude No.16 in B-Flat Minor
[17] Prelude No.17 in A-Flat
[18] Prelude No.18 in F Minor
[19] Prelude No.19 in E-Flat
[20] Prelude No.20 in C Minor
[21] Prelude No.21 in B-Flat
[22] Prelude No.22 in G Minor
[23] Prelude No.23 in F
[24] Prelude No.24 in D Minor

Sonata No.2 'Funeral March' in B-Flat Minor Op.35

[25] Grave: Doppio movimento

[26] Scherzo

[27] Marche funèbre: Lento

[28] Finale: Presto

[29] Polonaise in A-Flat Op.53

Evgeny Kissin, Piano

(P) 2000 BMG Music

ROBERT SCHUMANN

Sonata No.1 in F-Sharp Minor Op.11

[1] Introduzione (un poco Adagio); Allegro Vivace

[2] Aria: Senza passione, ma espressivo

[3] Scherzo e Intermezzo: Allegrissimo

[4] Finale: Allegro un poco maestoso

Carnaval Op.9

[5] Préambule

[6] Pierrot

[7] Arlequin

[8] Valse noble

[9] Eusebius

[10] Florestan

[11] Coquette

[12] Réplique

[13] Papillons

[14] ASCH – SCHA (Lettres dansantes)

[15] Chiarina

[16] Chopin

[17] Estrella
[18] Reconnaissance
[19] Pantalon et Colombine
[20] Valse allemande
[21] Paganini
[22] Aveu
[23] Promenade
[24] Pause
[25] Marche des 'Davidsbündler' contre les Philistins
Evgeny Kissin, Piano
(P) 2000 BMG Music

JOHANN SEBASTIAN BACH / FERRUCCIO BUSONI
Toccata, Adagio & Fugue in C BWV 564
[1] Prelude
[2] Intermezzo (Adagio)
[3] Fugue
MICHAIL GLINKA – ARR. MILY BALAKIREV
[4] The Lark
MODEST MUSSORGSKY Pictures at an Exhibition
[5] Promenade
[6] Gnomus
[7] Promenade
[8] Il vecchio castello
[9] Promenade
[10] Tuileries
[11] Bydlo
[12] Promenade

[13] Ballet of the Unhatched Chicks
[14] Samuel Goldenberg & Schmuÿle
[15] Promenade
[16] Limoges marché
[17] Catacombae (Sepulcrum romanum)
[18] Con mortuis in lingua mortua
[19] The Hut on Fowl's Legs (Baba-Yaga)
[20] The Great Gate of Kiev
Evgeny Kissin, Piano
(P) 2000 BMG Music

FRÉDÉRIC CHOPIN
[1] Ballade No.1 in G Minor Op.23
[2] Ballade No.2 in F Op.38
[3] Ballade No.3 in A-Flat Op.47
[4] Ballade No.4 in F Minor Op.52
[5] Berceuse in D-Flat Major Op.57
[6] Barcarolle in F-Sharp Major Op.60
[7] Scherzo No.4 in E Op.54
Evgeny Kissin, Piano
(P) 1999 BMG Music

JOHANN SEBASTIAN BACH / FERRUCCIO BUSONI
[1] Chaconne in D Minor
(Arr. from J.S. Bach's Partita No.2 for Violin BWV
    1004)
LUDWIG VAN BEETHOVEN
[2] Rondo in G Op.51 No.2

[3] Rondo a capriccio Op.129
'Rage over a Lost Penny'
ROBERT SCHUMANN
Kreisleriana Op.16
[4] Äußerst bewegt
[5] Sehr innig und nicht zu rasch
[6] Intermezzo I
[7] Intermezzo II
[8] Sehr aufgeregt: Etwas langsamer
[9] Sehr langsam: Etwas bewegter
[10] Sehr lebhaft
[11] Sehr langsam: Etwas bewegter
[12] Sehr rasch: Noch schneller
[13] Schnell und spielend
Evgeny Kissin, Piano
(P) 1998 BMG Music

LUDWIG VAN BEETHOVEN
Sonata 'Moonlight' Op.27 No.2
[1] Adagio sostenuto
[2] Allegretto
[3] Presto agitato
CÉSAR FRANCK
Prélude, Choral and Fugue
JOHANNES BRAHMS
Variations on a Theme of Paganini Op.35
Books I (Var. I–XIV) and II (Var. I–XIV)
Evgeny Kissin, Piano

(P) 1998 BMG Music

LUDWIG VAN BEETHOVEN
Concerto for Piano and Orchestra
No.2 in B-Flat Major Op.19
Concerto for Piano and Orchestra
No.5 'Emperor' in E-Flat Major Op.73
Evgeny Kissin, Piano
Philharmonia Orchestra
James Levine, Conductor
(P) 1997 Sony Music Entertainment

ROBERT SCHUMANN
Fantasy in C Op.17
[1] Durchaus phantastisch und leidenschaftlich vorzu-
    tragen
[2] Mäßig: Durchaus energisch
[3] Langsam getragen: Durchweg leise zu halten
FRANZ LISZT
Études d'exécution transcendante
[4] Chasse-neige (No.12)
[5] Harmonies du soir (No.11)
[6] In F Minor (No.10)
[7] Feux follets (No.5)
[8] Wilde Jagd (No.8)
Evgeny Kissin, Piano
(P) 1996 BMG Music
YEVGENY KISSIN

SCHUBERT: Wanderer-Fantasie D 760
BRAHMS: 7 Fantasien op. 116
LISZT: Ungarische Rhapsodie No. 12
Schubert-Lieder - Piano Transcriptions
Int. Release 03 Apr. 1995
0289 445 5622 3 CD DDD

JOSEPH HAYDN
[1] Piano Sonata in A Hob.XVI:30
Piano Sonata in E-Flat Major Hob.XVI:52
[2] Allegro
[3] Adagio
[4] Finale: Presto
FRANZ SCHUBERT
Piano Sonata in A Minor D.784
[5] Allegro giusto
[6] Andante
[7] Allegro vivace
FRANZ SCHUBERT / CARL TAUSIG
[8] Military March for Four Hands No.1 in D D.733
Evgeny Kissin, Piano
(P) 1995 Sony Music Entertainment

SERGE PROKOFIEV: Piano Concertos No. 1 op. 10,
    No. 3 op. 26
Yevgeny Kissin, Piano
Berliner Philharmoniker
Claudio Abbado, Conductor

Int. Release 05 Sep. 1994
0289 439 8982 4 CD DDD GH

FRÉDÉRIC CHOPIN
Piano Sonata No.3 in B Minor Op.58
[1] Allegro maestoso
[2] Scherzo
[3] Largo
[4] Finale: Presto, non tanto
[5] Mazurka in F Minor Op.63 No.2
[6] Mazurka in C Op.56 No.2
[7] Mazurka in C-Sharp Minor Op.63 No.3
[8] Mazurka in D-Flat Op.30 No.3
[9] Mazurka in F Minor Op.68 No.4
[10] Mazurka in G Op.50 No.1
[11] Mazurka in C-Sharp Minor Op.50 No.3
[12] Mazurka in D Op.33 No.2
[13] Mazurka in B-Flat Minor Op.24 No.4
[14] Mazurka in F-Sharp Minor Op.59 No.3
[15] Mazurka in A Minor Op.17 No.4
[16] Mazurka in B Op.63 No.1
Evgeny Kissin, Piano
Recorded live February 1993 at Carnegie Hall, New
    York City, USA
(P) 1994 BMG Music
FRÉDÉRIC CHOPIN
[1] Fantaisie in F Minor Op.49
[2] Waltz 'Grande valse' in A-Flat Op.42

[3] Waltz 'Grande valse brillante' in A Minor Op.34 No.2
[4] Waltz 'Grande valse brillante' in A-Flat Op.34 No.1
[5] Polonaise in F-Sharp Minor Op.44
[6] Nocturne in A-Flat Op.32 No.2
[7] Nocturne in C-Sharp Minor Op.27 No.1
[8] Nocturne in D-Flat Op.27 No.2
[9] Scherzo No.2 in B-Flat Minor Op.31
Evgeny Kissin, Piano
Recorded live February 1993 at Carnegie Hall, New York City, USA
(P) 1994 BMG Music

ROBERT SCHUMANN
Piano Concerto in A Minor Op.54
[1] Allegro affettuoso – Andante espressivo – Allegro (Tempo I)
[2] Intermezzo: Andantino grazioso
[3] Allegro vivace
Evgeny Kissin, Piano
Vienna Philharmonic Orchestra
Carlo Maria Giulini, Conductor
[4] Arabeske Op.18
FRANZ SCHUBERT / FRANZ LISZT
[5] Die Forelle
[6] Erlkönig
EDVARD GRIEG
[7] Fra karnevalet (Carnival Scene) Op.19 No.3
[8] Jeg elser dig (I Love You) Op.41 No.3

FRANZ LISZT

[9] Soirées de Vienne: Valse caprice No.6 S 427/6 (First
version) Nach Franz Schubert – Allegro con strepito
Evgeny Kissin, Piano
(P) 1993 Sony Music Entertainment

SERGEI RACHMANINOFF
Piano Concerto No.3 in D Minor Op.30
[1] Allegro ma non tanto
[2] Intermezzo: Adagio
[3] L'istesso tempo; Finale: Alla breve
Evgeny Kissin, Piano
Boston Symphony Orchestra
Seiji Ozawa, Conductor
Songs Op.34
[4] Vocalise No.14 (Arr.Richardson)
[5] Prelude in B-Flat Op.23 No.2
Evgeny Kissin, Piano
(P) 1993 BMG Music

WOLFGANG AMADEUS MOZART
Piano Concerto No.20 in D Minor K.466
[1] Allegro
[2] Romance
[3] Rondo: Allegro assai
[4] Rondo in D K.382
Piano Concerto No.12 in A K.414
[5] Allegro

[6] Andante
[7] Allegretto
Evgeny Kissin, Piano
Moscow Virtuosi
Vladimir Spivakov, Conductor
(P) 1992 BMG Music

BEETHOVEN IN BERLIN
The New Year's Eve Concert 1991
Musik zu 'Egmont' Op. 84
'Ah! perfido' Op. 65
Ouvertüre 'Leonore III' Op. 72a
Fantasie für Klavier, Chor und Orchester op. 80
Yevgeny Kissin, Piano
Cheryl Studer, Soprano
Bruno Ganz, Recitation
RIAS-Kammerchor · Berliner Philharmoniker
Claudio Abbado, Conductor
Int. Release 10 Feb. 1992

SERGEI PROKOFIEV
Sonata No.6 in A Op.82
[1] Allegro moderato
[2] Allegretto
[3] Tempo di valzer lentissimo
[4] Vivace
FRANZ LISZT
[5] Liebestraum No.3

[6] Rhapsodie espagnole
FRÉDÉRIC CHOPIN
[7] Waltz in C-Sharp Minor Op.64 No.2
FRANZ LISZT
[8] Transcendental Étude No.10 in F Minor
ROBERT SCHUMANN / FRANZ LISZT
[9] Widmung
SERGEI PROKOFIEV
[10] Étude in C Minor Op.2 No.3
Evgeny Kissin, Piano
(P) 1990 BMG Music

ROBERT SCHUMANN
[1] Variations on the name Abegg Op.1
Symphonic Études Op.13
[2] Theme 1
[3] Variation I
[4] Posthumous variation I
[5] Variation II
[6] Variation III
[7] Variation IV
[8] Variation V
[9] Variation VI
[10] Posthumous variation IV
[11] Posthumous variation V
[12] Variation VII
[13] Posthumous variation III
[14] Variation VIII

[15] Variation IX

[16] Posthumous variation II

[17] Variation X

[18] Variation XI

[19] Finale

Evgeny Kissin, Piano

(P) 1990 BMG Music

SERGEI RACHMANINOFF

[1] Lilacs

Études Tableaux Op.39

[2] No.5 in E-Flat Minor

[3] No.1 in C Minor

SERGEI PROKOFIEV

Sonata No.6 in A Op.82

[4] I. Allegro moderato

[5] II. Allegretto

[6] III. Tempo di valzer lentissimo

[7] IV. Vivace

FRANZ LISZT

[8] Trois Études de Concert: 'La leggierezza' No.2 in F Minor

[9] Zwei Konzertetuden: 'Waldesrauschen' No.1 in D-Flat Major

FRÉDÉRIC CHOPIN

[10] Nocturne in A-Flat Major Op.32 No.2

[11] Polonaise in F-Sharp Minor Op.44

[12] Mazurka in E Minor Op.25

ALEXANDER SCRIABIN
[13] Étude in C-Sharp Minor Op.42 No.5
Encores
SAKUNOSUKE KOY AMA
[14] Natu-Wa Kinu
TRADITIONAL
[15] Todai-Mori (Lighthouse Keeper)
[16] Usagi (Rabbit)
Evgeny Kissin, Piano
(P) 1990 Sony Music Entertainment

JOSEPH HAYDN
Piano Concerto in D Hob.XVIII:11
[1] Vivace
[2] Un poco adagio
[3] Rondo all'ungherese: Allegro assai
Evgeny Kissin, Piano
Moscow Virtuosi
Vladimir Spivakov, Conductor
DMITRI SHOSTAKOVI CH
Piano Concerto No.1 in C Minor Op.35
[4] Allegro moderato
[5] Lento
[6] Moderato
[7] Allegro brio: Presto
Evgeny Kissin, Piano
Vassili Kan, Trumpet
Moscow Virtuosi

Vladimir Spivakov, Conductor
SERGEI PROKOFIEV
[8] Overture on Hebrew Themes Op.34
Vladimir Spivakov, Boris Garlitski, Piano
Yuri Gandelsman, Viola
Mikhail Milman, Cello
Evgeny Kissin, Piano
Michel Lethiec, Clarinet
(P) 1990 BMG Music

ALEXANDER SCRIABIN
4 Pieces for Piano Op. 51
Étude Op. 42 No. 5
PETER TCHAIKOVSKY
Piano Concerto No. 1
Yevgeny Kissin, Piano
Berliner Philharmoniker
Herbert von Karajan, Conductor
Int. Release 01 Sep. 1989

SERGEI RACHMANINOFF
Concerto No.2 in C Minor Op.18
[1] Moderato: Allegro
[2] Adagio sostenuto
[3] Allegro scherzando
Evgeny Kissin, Piano
London Symphony Orchestra
Valery Gergiev, Conductor

Études-tableaux Op.39
[4] No.1 in C Minor
[5] No.2 in A Minor
[6] No.4 in B Minor
[7] No.5 in E-Flat Minor
[8] No.6 in A Minor
[9] No.9 in D
Evgeny Kissin, Piano
(P) 1988 BMG Music

Video

YEVGENY KISSIN
Works by Schubert – Brahms – Liszt – Bach – Gluck/
  Sgambati
Directed by Christopher Nupen
Int. Release 01 Feb. 2008
A production of Concerto Winderstein, Munich